So What . . . About Copyright?

What Artists Need to Know About Copyright & Trademarks

For filmmakers, visual artists, and writers

● ● ● ● ● ● ● ● ● ● ● ● ● ● ● ●

Edited by
David Bollier, Gigi Bradford,
Laurie Racine and Gigi B. Sohn

Produced by PUBLIC KNOWLEDGE
"The public's voice in the digital age."

Published by **Public Knowledge**

Public Knowledge

First Edition

Library of Congress Catalog Number:
ISBN: 1-4116-5379-3

Printed in the United States of America

PREFACE

Why Would You Read This Book?

> "Overprotecting intellectual property is as harmful as underprotecting it. Culture is impossible without a rich public domain. Nothing today, likely nothing since we tamed fire, is genuinely new: Culture, like science and technology, grows by accretion, each new creator building on the works of those who came before. Overprotection stifles the very creative forces it's supposed to nurture."
>
> *Alex Kozinski, Judge, Ninth Circuit Court of Appeals*

The post-industrial global world is based on ideas and creativity. Raw materials and industry are no longer the main engines of economic growth. Ideas and inventions zip around the world at lightning speed and have changed the way that we communicate, entertain, copy, produce, and prosper.

More and more, our courts are being asked to weigh whether art and culture are the result of various discrete "Eureka" moments or the accumulation of new ways to interpret ageless emotions and questions. The laws we employ to nourish innovation and protect creation have changed. Some wonder if new restrictions hinder creative expression. Could it be the great intellectual land grab of our time? Is it the fencing of the prairie of ideas? Are the established gaining ground at the expense of the emerging?

It's time for artists to understand their existing rights and how those rights may be shrinking. The stakes are enormous. Creators need to know how the public domain – the store of words, sounds, images, and other memories that are free for all to use or build upon – is being corralled. When thinking about copyright, most people focus on protecting completed expression. This is an important part of copyright and has always been so. But what once was the equal half of the equation is shrinking: the ability to tap into to a rich public domain available to all.

Read this book. It will lay out in plain and accessible language the social balance written into the U.S. Constitution between access to content in the public domain and control over personal art and expression. It could change what you think is important. It could help you to protect your future work and your ability to make that work in a world that increasingly values, and tries to control, creativity and innovation in this century.

Gigi Bradford
Washington, DC
2005

How To Use This Book

Who this book is for and what this book is about:

So What . . .About Copyright? is designed for artists, authors, and scholars of all kinds. It comprises a series of essays written with the creator in mind. The book is framed by a comprehensive overview chapter and then supported by subsequent chapters targeted to different creative groups – filmmakers, visual artists, and writers. It attempts to give you a theoretical and practical understanding of the important and evolving concepts that make up copyright, trademark, fair use, and the public domain. Today's world relies more and more on creativity and on ideas. Consequently, courts and legislators are increasingly being asked to interpret intellectual property laws, many of which have changed a great deal in the last thirty years. Anyone who creates art or ideas and who values both intellectual property and the viability of a robust public domain will benefit from reading this clear and user-friendly book.

What this book is not about:

So What. . . is **not** designed to provide legal advice. It **is** designed to give readers an understanding of the historic balance between copyright and the public domain as it was written into the U. S. Constitution; how copyright and trademark laws have evolved over time; what they are intended to accomplish; and how you can make sure you understand, benefit from, and follow them. This book is not a how-to or a practical compendium, but rather a clear explanation of a topic that can appear so complex that those who need to know about it often avoid the topic altogether.

How this book is organized:

Begin with the overview section and the conclusion. Then, delve into sections that are targeted to specific creative genres – filmmaking, visual arts, and writing. Don't forget to read the conclusion. It will tell you why these changing legal concepts are vitally important to you now. It will suggest ways to stay informed and will help you decide how you want to consider your own rights.

CONTRIBUTORS
SO WHAT… ABOUT COPYRIGHT?
What Artists Need to Know About Copyright & Trademarks
For filmmakers, visual artists, and writers
Produced by PUBLIC KNOWLEDGE
"The public's voice in the digital age."

WHY WOULD YOU READ THIS BOOK?	*Gigi Bradford*
HOW TO USE THIS BOOK:	*Gigi Bradford*
OVERVIEW:	*Jessica Litman, Kay Murray, Christine Steiner* "What Every Artist Should Know About Copyright and Trademark Law"
VISUAL ARTS:	*Christine Steiner* "Visual Arts and Intellectual Property"
FILMMAKERS:	*Vivian Kleiman and Gretchen Stoeltje* "Picking the Lock: Filmmaking in the Digital Age"
WRITERS:	*Kay Murray* "Copyright, Contracts, & Publishing Realities for Authors"
CONCLUSION:	*Gigi B. Sohn*
EDITORS:	*David Bollier, Gigi Bradford, Laurie Racine and Gigi Sohn*

- *Jessica Litman is author of many publications including <u>Digital Copyright.</u> She teaches at Wayne State University Law School.*
- *Vivian Kleiman is an award-winning documentary filmmaker and Adjunct Professor at Stanford University; Gretchen Stoeltje is an independent filmmaker expert in legal issues.*
- *Christine Steiner is an attorney based in Los Angeles whose cutting-edge concepts and publications addressing intellectual property and copyright issues for visual artists and museums have achieved national and international recognition. Research assistance provided by Valerie Geyber & Sarah Conley.*
- *Kay Murray is General Counsel and Assistant Director of the Writers Guild. She is coauthor of <u>The Writer's Legal Guide.</u>*
- *David Bollier is a co-founder of Public Knowledge, the author of <u>Brand Name Bullies: The Quest to Own and Control Culture</u>, and the Editor of OntheCommons.org.*
- *Gigi Bradford has worked in arts and culture for over 25 years and is an editor of <u>The Politics of Culture</u>.*
- *Laurie Racine is the co-founder and Chair of Public Knowledge. She is also Chair of Doc Arts, Inc and Teacher's Without Borders.*
- *Gigi B. Sohn is President of Public Knowledge, an organization that advocates a balanced approach to copyright and technology policy.*

The opinions expressed herein are those of the individual writers and are not intended to provide legal advice or counsel.

ACKNOWLEDGEMENTS

So What . . . About Copyright? What Artists Need to Know About Copyright & Trademarks is supported by the Center for the Public Domain and by grants from the Nathan Cummings Foundation, The Rockefeller Foundation, and the Andy Warhol Foundation for the Visual Arts.

Public Knowledge, *"the public's voice in the digital age,"* is a public-interest advocacy organization dedicated to fortifying and defending a vibrant information commons. This publication is part of its *Empowering Creators in the Digital Age* project, which is designed to address how digital technologies and restrictive copyright policies affect the ability of artists to create.

Public Knowledge is:

Gigi B. Sohn, President
Mike Godwin, Legal Director
Art Brodsky, Communications Director
Alex Curtis, Government Affairs Manager
Peter Suber, Director, Open Access Project
Scott Burns, Staff Technologist
Ann Oliverio, Office Manager

Public Knowledge would also like to thank Nathan Mitchler, its former Intellectual Property Counsel, and Jef Pearlman and Heidi Wachs, its 2004 Summer Law Clerks, for providing valuable assistance with this project.

Public Knowledge Board of Directors:

Hal Abelson
David Bollier, Secretary
Reed Hundt, Treasurer
Lawrence Lessig
Jonathan Taplin
Laurie Racine, Chair
Gigi B. Sohn, President

Empowering Creators Project Director: Gigi Bradford
Publications Director: Stacey Mewborn
Printer: LuLu Enterprises

TABLE OF CONTENTS

"What Every Artist Should Know About Copyright and Trademark Law"

OVERVIEW

Jessica Litman, Kay Murray, and Christine Steiner

INTELLECTUAL PROPERTY & YOU

Patent, copyright, trademark and trade secrecy are species of *intellectual property*, which is a legal right to control and license a tangible mental creation. Intellectual property rights – particularly copyright and trademark – have always been important for artists, authors, composers, musicians, filmmakers, painters, sculptors and other creators. They enable creators to earn money from the works they create while generating new art, knowledge, and information for the public.

Intellectual property is a legal right to control and license a tangible mental creation.

This primer focuses on copyright and trademark law. Copyright and trademark are different concepts, protecting different types of property through different enforcement mechanisms. Both are mechanisms of legal control created by Congress and enforced by the courts; both have registration schemes that offer distinct advantages; both have established fair use principles; and both are widely misunderstood.

Since all writing, music, and art echoes and sometimes incorporates the creative expression of earlier authors, intellectual property protection potentially impedes new creativity and discourages authors from making their work available to the public. This primer seeks to help you understand your legal rights and obligations under copyright and trademark law and how these realities may affect your work as an artist.

Copyrights and trademarks are like physical property in the sense that they can be owned, sold, leased, and borrowed. Intellectual property rights are both similar to and different from your rights in a house, a car, a sweater, or a turkey sandwich. Calling copyright and trademarks "property" gives us information about some of their characteristics – in this case, that they can be licensed, bought and sold. But copyright and trademark have other important characteristics, such as limited terms and public usage rights, which make them very different from tangible property.

COPYRIGHT Overview
Copyright Defined

A *copyright* is a form of protection provided to authors of original works of authorship including literary, dramatic, musical, artistic, choreographic, architectural and audiovisual works.

Copyright Highlights

- Copyright protection is automatic.
- Copyrights are limited in both time and scope.
- Copyright protects your "expression," but not your ideas or the facts that you express.

How Copyright Is Created

Copyright protection is automatic. A copyright springs into being as soon as you create a copyrightable work and "fix" it in tangible form by writing it down or recording it. The copyright will only protect material that is original to you. If you photograph the Golden Gate Bridge, your copyright will automatically protect your photograph insofar as it embodies your expression of the way the bridge looks. However, your copyright will give you no rights to stop other people from taking their own photographs of the Golden Gate Bridge.

Limitations of Copyrights

Copyrights are limited in both time and scope. The Constitution requires that copyrights endure for "limited times." Congress has set that duration at the length of the author's life plus 70 years or 95 years for older works and works made for hire. Copyrights give authors exclusive rights in particular uses of their works. The public has rights in copyrighted works, however, free of the copyright owner's control. For example, copyright law gives the copyright owner the exclusive right to perform the copyrighted work *publicly* or to authorize others to do so. It does not, however, give the copyright owner any right to control *private* performances. Copyrights may be sold or otherwise transferred, but the law requires that any transfer of copyright ownership be reflected in a signed, written contract.

> The duration of copyright is life of the author plus 70 years, or 95 years for works made for hire and older works.

The Purpose of Copyright

Contrary to popular opinion, the purpose of copyright is not to give authors or publishers control over their works. The copyright system exists to ensure that we have a wide variety of creative works available to consume, enjoy, learn from and use. In the 18th Century language of the United States

Constitution, the purpose of copyright is to "Promote the Progress of Science." The first United States copyright law was titled *An Act for the Encouragement of Learning*. The primary purpose of copyright law is to advance and spread knowledge. In that regard, most people would agree that the American copyright law has been fabulously successful.

The copyright system is also designed to encourage artists and others to create new works. In theory, if you give every author a copyright in every work she creates, she can sell the copyright to a distributor, who will pay her money for the right to distribute her work to the rest of us. In practice, though, most distributors don't pay most creators very much. That isn't necessarily because record companies or book publishers, for example, are exploiting creators, but partly because most means of mass dissemination have required significant capital investments until recently. Historically, to transform a work of authorship into something that could be used by the public, and to get that work into people's homes, has required printing presses, paper, warehouses, trains, trucks, and broadcast towers. Copyright law was designed to make it easy for distributors to recoup their expenses and earn profits on distribution. This gives publishers, record labels and film studios strong incentives to invest in the distribution of works of authorship – sometimes to the detriment of individual creators.

Today, traditional distribution is still expensive, but we also have relatively new methods of digital distribution that are less costly and more efficient. This development makes it all the more important that we strike the right balance in copyright law between public access to creative works and the creator's ability to control and profit from his works. Several legal and other mechanisms provide that balance. One of the most important is the public domain.

The Public Domain

The public domain is a realm of information and culture where intellectual property protection does not apply. When copyrights and patents expire, innovations and creative works enter the public domain. Some works - such as facts and government documents - are not eligible for copyright and automatically are considered in the pub-

> The public domain is a realm of information and culture where intellectual property protection does not apply.

Selected List of Items in the Public Domain

- Patented and copyrighted works/inventions for which the term of protection has expired. This encompasses all copyrighted works published before 1923.
- Facts.
- Mathematical/scientific formulas, laws of nature.
- Government works – The U.S. government may not copyright works.
- Disclaimer of Rights – Works whose owners have relinquished their rights under the law.
- Laws, court opinions, regulations.

How to Put Works in the Public Domain

For a number of reasons, artists may wish to donate their works to be freely used, reproduced, distributed, etc. For more on Creative Commons, see p. 33. before the term of copyright expires. Although a copyright holder may choose not to enforce her rights, this alone does not make the work "available" or in the public domain. For instance, someone wishing to use the work cannot easily verify the creator's intent, and heirs may later choose to enforce copyrights. The key is making sure that people who encounter the work are aware that certain or unlimited uses are permitted.

The easiest way to put a work into the Public Domain is by including a clear notice or licensing term with the work. This notice or license should clearly state that the copyright holder wishes to donate the work to the public domain and that she permits all uses of the work. For the first time, there is now an easy mechanism for placing works in the public domain. The Creative Commons (www.creativecommons.org) offers a variety of licenses that make it easy for creators to choose how they may wish to define their intellectual property rights – including placing their works in the public domain.

lic domain. Anything in the public domain may be used by anyone without permission and without the payment of a licensing fee. The public domain is a treasure trove of information, resources, and inspiration that artists and creators constantly use to make new works.

Fair Use

The Copyright Act sets forth the exclusive rights that you have in your creations. It provides the rules for licensing rights, the remedies for infringement, and the procedure for litigating infringement suits. Federal courts interpret every aspect of the Act and have major influence over how the law works in real life.

More information on fair use and how to determine your rights as related to fair use is provided on page 20.

The Copyright Act also stipulates exceptions to these exclusive rights. One of the major exceptions is the doctrine of *fair use*. Fair use is an important concept, especially for artists, because it permits a creator to use copyrighted materials without permission, where the use is in the public interest.

Copyright Law EXPLAINED
Qualifying for Copyright

To qualify for copyright, a work must be original and fixed in a tangible form. It need not be published or registered to be copyrighted. The moment you put your words on paper (or in an e-mail, tape recorder, or other discernible medium), they are fully protected. Copyright protection is automatic. It doesn't matter in what material object you fix your work. If you want to fix your short stories by pasting letters cut out from the newspaper on your floor, that's okay. Video games and computer programs are fixed in computer chips – that's okay too. All that's required is a fairly permanent, tangible embodiment that will permit the work to be perceived, with or without the aid of a machine.

To be "original," the work must contain a grain of creativity. The amount of creativity required, however, is modest. The white pages of a metropolitan phone book listing every resident in alphabetical order are not original enough for copyright protection, but the material commonly included in phone books as front matter, which presents information about the phone company service and the local community, typically shows enough originality to qualify.

What Copyright Protects

Copyright does not protect every element in any copyrighted work. The law protects your "expression," but not your ideas or the facts that you express. Ideas and facts (including procedures, general themes, stock characters, processes, systems, concepts, principles and discoveries), no matter how unique, are not protected by copyright. Names, titles, slogans and short phrases are not copyrightable, but might be covered by trademark.

> Copyright does not protect every element in any copyrighted work.

Derivative Works & Compilations

When you create a work that uses, copies, or incorporates a preexisting work, your contribution is automatically protected by copyright as long as your use of the preexisting work is lawful. Your new work is called a "derivative work," and its copyright protects only the new elements.

●●● Scenario:

Shakespeare's *Richard III* is in the public domain, so anyone can adapt it. If you were to translate it into 21st Century vernacular, you would be entitled to copyright protection for your version. However, the copyright wouldn't give you any rights to restrict someone else from using the original Shakespeare. If a literature professor were to write a new scholarly preface to Shakespeare's *Richard III* and copiously annotate the text with scholarly comments, her copyright would protect only her preface and comments.

For more information on derivative works, refer to Adaptation on page 29.

If you collect preexisting elements into an anthology, collage, or collection, the selection and arrangement of the preexisting elements are protected as a "compilation." Again, your copyright covers only your additions, not the original works.

▪ Registering Your Copyright

Registration of copyright is optional, although you must register before you file a copyright infringement suit. Because registration is inexpensive (the fee is currently $30) and confers significant advantages in court, you should consider registering your copyright in any works that have meaningful commercial potential. You can find instructions for registering your copyrights on the United States Copyright Office website at http://www.copyright.gov.

Real World Example: *Rocky IV*

What if your use of preexisting material is "unlawful"? Recent court cases have held that copyright does not protect a derivative work if the derivative author's use of the underlying work amounted to copyright infringement. In *Anderson v. Stallone*, a screenwriter created a treatment for a sequel to *Rocky*, sent it to Sylvester Stallone, and actually met with executives at MGM to discuss the treatment. MGM never followed up. When it released *Rocky IV*, the screenwriter concluded that the movie had been based on his treatment and filed a copyright infringement suit.

He lost – not just because the court concluded that *Rocky IV* wasn't based on his treatment, but also because he didn't have permission to write the treatment in the first place. The court held that the screenwriter's treatment, created on spec and without permission from Stallone or MGM, infringed the copyrights in the first three *Rocky* movies. Since he didn't have permission, the screenwriter had used copyrighted elements of the *Rocky* movies "unlawfully," and therefore, his treatment was ineligible for copyright protection.[1]

When You Don't Need Permission

You don't always need permission before you may use copyrighted material to create a derivative work or a compilation. Sometimes there's a privilege granted by law; sometimes your use of the work is lawful because of fair use. Parodies are a familiar example. They are often (but not always) allowed under fair use. But if you don't seek permission, or are unable to secure it, there is a risk that you will lose copyright protection for that portion of your derivative work or compilation that incorporates copyrighted material without permission.

FAIR USE & Copyright

Fair use strives to ensure that an author's exclusive bundle of property rights will not hinder the very creativity the law was designed to foster. The doctrine recognizes that new works draw inspiration from older works and that productive use of older works promotes the progress of science, the arts, and literature. Fair use permits someone to use copyrighted materials without permission where the use is in the public interest. The law specifically mentions criticism, comment, news reporting, teaching, scholarship, and research as exemplary fair uses, but there is no clear-cut rule. Fair use is determined on a case-by-case basis. An activity may qualify in one instance as fair use, while it would be an infringing activity in another context.

> Fair use is determined on a case-by-case basis. An activity may qualify in one instance as fair use, while it would be an infringing activity in another context.

The Fair Use Factors

In determining fair use, the copyright law sets forth four factors to be applied. These factors are outlined in the following table.

These criteria cannot be evaluated in isolation as a mathematical formulation. Rather, the test is the "totality of the circumstances." Although the flexibility inherent in the test often leaves users and providers unsure of whether the contemplated use is a fair use, these factors guide the courts in making case-by-case determinations. The four factors are described below in detail.

The Four Fair Use Factors

1. The purpose and type (or "character") of the use, including whether such use is of a commercial nature or is for nonprofit educational purposes;
2. The type of copyrighted work;
3. The amount and substantiality of the portion used in relation to the copyrighted work as a whole; and
4. The effect of the use upon the potential market for or value of the copyrighted work.

1. The Purpose and Type of Use

Uses of a work that are "transformative," and not merely duplicative, are more likely to be considered fair use. Transformative use means that the new work does more than simply recast the original work to create a derivative work.[2] Instead, the creator uses the underlying work to make a different work that stands on its own as an original expression. This is seen as advancing the policy goals of copyright – to promote and disseminate knowledge. Generally speaking, not-for-profit uses are more likely to be held fair than for-profit uses.[3]

Real World Example: *The Wind Done Gone*

In a recent case,[4] Alice Randall's book *The Wind Done Gone*, based on Margaret Mitchell's *Gone With the Wind*, was found to be a transformative work. Despite the fact that the author of *The Wind Done Gone* used many of the original characters and story line, the court found that *The Wind Done Gone* transformed these elements in order to comment on the original work.[5]

2. Type of Copyrighted Work

In assessing whether a work is a fair use, courts also consider whether a copyrighted work is likely to be built upon and disseminated broadly. Thus, less copyright protection is given to factual works (*e.g.,* scholarly or scientific works) than to creative works (paintings, novels, films). A court will also consider whether a work is unpublished in order to recognize an author's right to first publication. But use of an unpublished work may be considered a fair use, depending on the four-factor analysis. By contrast, European law protects an artist's absolute right to determine when and how a work is published.

3. The Amount and Substantiality Used

In determining whether fair use is appropriate, a court will consider the amount and substantiality of what has been copied from the underlying work. The court may consider what proportion of the work has been copied and/or how important the copied portion is to the work as a whole.[6] That is, the analysis is both a quantitative and qualitative one, examining how much is too much. A work of visual art is generally viewed as a whole and borrowing "more than necessary" is often difficult to assess. Using an entire work does not necessarily mean that the new use is not a fair one because the courts weigh all four factors.

4.   The Effect of the Use Upon the Potential Market

This final factor in determining whether the use of another's copyrighted work qualifies as fair is the commercial impact. A copyright owner may object that a use hurts the market for his work. The owner need not show actual harm; potential harm is sufficient to invalidate a fair use.[7]

Real World Example: *Photocopies of Scientific & Technical Journals*

Texaco was sued for its practice of photocopying and internally redistributing articles from commercial scientific and technical journals. The court found that although there was no established market for sales of individual articles, it was still "appropriate that potential licensing revenues for photocopying be considered in a fair use analysis." The court, relying on the fourth fair use criterion, ruled that the photocopying had unfairly deprived the copyright holder of potential licensing revenue (the potential market), and secondarily, of potentially increased subscription rates (the existing market).

Real World Example: *Napster*

In deciding whether or not the users of Napster's digital music sharing service were engaged in fair use, a federal court cited the Supreme Court's assertion that the fourth factor was the most important factor, but said that the standards for finding commercial harm could vary with the nature of the use. For non-commercial use, for example, the party alleging infringement must show that "either the particular use is harmful, or that if it should become widespread, it would adversely affect the potential market for the copyrighted work." Moreover, just because an established market is not harmed does not mean that the copyright holder loses "the right to develop alternative markets for the works." In the Napster case, the court found that Napster both decreased sales of the copyrighted works among certain users (hurting the current market for purchased music), and that it also raised the barrier to entry for online music sales by copyright owners (hurting potential future markets). Thus, the court found that Napster users were not engaged in fair use.

Parody As A Type of Fair Use

There is generally no hard and fast rule as to what constitutes fair use. There are some generally accepted categories of uses that are usually considered "fair," although one should always consider the four factors in making a final determination.

Parody is frequently attacked by copyright holders not only because it uses their works without authorization, but because it makes fun of them. But parody is not simple copying; it is a transformative use. A work parodying another usually takes distinguishing features of the original work to make a clear association between the original and the parody, and then exploits this association to comment on the original work.

Determining whether a parody is fair use can require some highly subjective and fact-intensive analysis. But to provide some general parameters, the courts have attempted to craft some guidelines. From the court cases decided to date, several elements emerge. For a parody to be considered fair use:

1. It must comment on the original work;
2. It should use only as much of the original material as is needed and not enough to confuse the consumer or public or dilute the commercial value of the original; and
3. It should not seek to replace the original in the marketplace.

When copyrighted material is used in parody, courts generally apply the four fair use factors. Perhaps the most important and controversial consideration to be made in determining the difference between infringement and fair use is whether the parody, in making its point, comments on the original work.[8] Courts have held consistently that where there does not appear to be a specific link between the comment being made and the original work, then the argument for fair use is weak.[9]

Real World Example: *"Oh, Pretty Woman"*

In *Campbell v. Acuff-Rose Music*, the owners of the copyright in Roy Orbison's song, "Oh, Pretty Woman," sued the rap group 2 Live Crew, claiming that the group's parody song infringed their copyright by using the first line of the lyrics and the song's opening bass riff. The Supreme Court found that because 2 Live Crew's song was a "transformative" work (one which greatly alters the original), added significant amounts of new material, and criticized the work it transformed, it qualified as a fair use. The court reached this conclusion even though 2 Live Crew was using those portions of the copyrighted work for commercial purposes. Why? Because the critical and transformative nature of the parody made it unlikely to serve as a substitute for the original in the marketplace.

Real World Example: *The Cat NOT in the Hat!*

The owners of most of Dr. Seuss's copyrights sued the author of a book titled *The Cat NOT in the Hat! A Parody by Dr. Juice* for copyright infringement. *The Cat NOT in the Hat!* told the story of the O.J. Simpson murder trial in the style of Dr. Seuss. The court found that the work was not a parody, but a satire. The book did not criticize Dr. Seuss through the use of his distinctive style and elements of his copyrighted works (which would constitute a parody), but instead appropriated them for an entirely different purpose, to tell the story of the trial (which constitutes a satire). The court held that *The Cat NOT in the Hat!* was not transformative, and was a commercial expression, and there for it was not considered a fair use.

Real World Example: *Annie Liebovitz v. Paramount Pictures*

Annie Liebovitz sued Paramount for advertising one of their movies using an image which closely resembled Liebovitz's famous photograph of a pregnant Demi Moore. Paramount's version of the photograph was lit and posed in the same fashion as the original, but instead of the original woman's serious expression, the studio had superimposed actor Leslie Nielsen's smirking face on a women's body. The court found that because the Paramount photograph criticized the serious nature of the Liebovitz's photo, and did not serve as a market substitute for the original photo, it qualified as a parody that is protected as fair use.

Parody v. Satire

A parody generally imitates or mimics a style or look, while a satire is often a humorous or political critique of a vice or error. The difference between each is subtle, but important because the law of fair use protects parody, but does not protect satire. A parody can be a satire, but many satires are not considered parodies. Common examples of satires include the comic strip *Doonesbury*, the writings of Al Franken, *The Onion*, and many of Weird Al Yankovic's songs. Unlike a parody, a satire does not necessarily comment on the original copyrighted material it uses. For instance, an infringing satire might utilize the style or elements of a copyrighted painting to comment on politics or promote human rights. But because such satires do not comment on the original painting, they would not qualify as a parody protected by fair use.

New Technology

The Copyright Act has many specific, detailed exemptions and privileges, most of which are beyond the scope of this primer. Fair use is one of the few general privileges. But what happens when a new technology arrives on the scene? The law is structured so that new technology is presumptively covered on the same terms and conditions as preexisting technology. New technology usually doesn't fit into a specific exemption because Congress obviously could not anticipate all new technologies when it undertook the last major rewrite of the Copyright Act, in 1976. Since then, consumer videotaping, digital audio recording, satellite television, personal computers, and the Internet have become pervasive technologies, creating new tensions between their users and the law. Usually, new technology users invoke the fair use exemption to justify their uses of these new media. Courts have needed to decide when and under what circumstances uses of these technologies should be deemed fair use.

Real World Example: *The VCR*

●●●●●●●●●●●●●●●●●●

The most famous fair use case in the 20th Century was *Sony Corp. of America v. Universal City Studios,*[10] in which the Supreme Court held that using a VCR to record television programs to watch them later was fair use. Courts have also held that copies made of software during reverse engineering of computer programs can be fair use.[11]

Watch Out For: **Peer-to-Peer (P2P) Networks**

One of the core principles of the *Sony* VCR case was that a manufacturer could not be held legally responsible for illegal uses of a technology if such technology is capable of "substantial non-infringing uses." Because the VCR can be used for legitimate as well as unlawful purposes, the Supreme Court refused to find VCR manufacturers liable for any copyright infringement engaged in by VCR owners.

This principle is now being tested in the courts as a result of the enormous growth of new commercial "peer-to-peer" file-sharing (P2P) networks. Individuals who download P2P software connect their computers directly to others who have done the same, and as a result can share none, some or all of the files on their hard drives. These networks have raised the ire of the record and movie companies, as well as some artists, who see these networks as nothing but tools for copyright infringement. Other companies and artists use these wildly popular networks to sell and distribute copies of their works and to track what songs are currently popular.

Currently, the record and movie companies are in a legal battle with Grokster, a distributor of peer-to-peer file sharing software. As in the *Sony* case, the companies are arguing that Grokster and its ilk should be held responsible for illegal uses of its technology. Basing its decision solely on the *Sony* principle, a federal trial court and a federal appeals court found for Grokster on the basis that P2P technology is capable of "substantial non-infringing uses." However, the United States Supreme Court ruled in favor of the companies, finding that although P2P technology is not illegal, there was significant evidence that Grokster's business model encouraged or "induced" copyright infringement. [12] The case will now go back to the trial court to determine whether there is enough evidence to find Grokster guilty of "secondary" copyright liability because it induced infringement.

Real World Example: *Napster and Grokster*

Why did a federal court find Napster liable for copyright infringement, but not Grokster? Aren't they both file sharing networks? They are, but their underlying technologies are very different, which is why Napster was effectively destroyed while P2P networks like Grokster still survive, at least for now. Napster used a centralized storage system for music files, maintained lists of shared files, provided technical support, and otherwise had the ability to control the activities of its users once its software was installed on their machines. Grokster and similar P2P software distributors have no such control; they simply distribute their software and let users do the rest.

Resources that Can Help Determine Fair Use

University of Texas Crash Course in Copyright
http://www.utsystem.edu/ogc/intellectualproperty/cprtindx.htm#top

Stanford Copyright & Fair Use Center
http://fairuse.stanford.edu/

Copyright Management Center
http://www.copyright.iupui.edu

University of Maryland Copyright and Fair Use Guidelines
http://www.umuc.edu/library/copy.html

The Copyright Primer (University of Maryland University College)
http://www-apps.umuc.edu/primer/enter.php#

Exclusive Rights

The copyright law defines exclusive rights for copyright owners in broad terms and then specifies specific exceptions. These exclusive rights are:

1. Reproduction – the right to copy
2. Adaptation – the right to make derivative works
3. Distribution – the right to distribute copies
4. Public Performance – the right to perform publicly
5. Public Display – the right to display publicly

In addition, the owners of sound recording copyrights, which don't include a general public performance right, have a limited digital performance right.

Use of a copyrighted work is not infringing unless it invades one of the exclusive rights in the copyright law. Even if the use of a work comes within an exclusive right, that use may still be lawful if it is covered by one of the many exceptions set out in the law. Only the copyright owner may exercise these rights or authorize others to do so. The rights can overlap.

⦿⦿⦿ Scenario:

If a publisher decides to publish an unauthorized illustrated version of a novel, it is violating the exclusive right to make copies, the right to create derivative works, and the right to distribute copies. An act that violates only one of the rights is still infringing. If a bookstore sells a couple of these illustrated versions to customers, it is infringing the copyright by violating only the right to distribute copies.

1. Reproduction

The right to make copies is the fundamental copyright right. It's why we call it a *copy*right law rather than, say, an *authors' rights* law. The reproduction right covers verbatim copies, photocopies, and the creation of new works that copy protected expression. It has been well settled since the 19th Century that copying is copying, whether conscious or not. Indeed, many music copyright infringement cases are about subconscious, rather than conscious copying.

Jerome Kern got into trouble in 1924 for subconsciously copying a bass line he had once heard.[13] Alex Haley was sued over his book *Roots* by someone who alleged that he had subconsciously copied her book.[14]

● ● ● **Scenario:**

If Karen writes a novel and Leonard steals the manuscript and makes copies, Leonard is violating Karen's reproduction right. If, instead, Leonard writes a novel but copies the plot, characters, and some of the language from Karen, he is still violating the reproduction right. If Leonard sells his infringing manuscript to a publisher who prints 5000 copies, the publisher is infringing Karen's reproduction right even though the publisher has no reason to know that Leonard copied Karen's novel.

2. Adaptation

The second exclusive right of copyright law is the right to create derivative works. This is the right to adapt a work. A derivative work is a new work that is based on the old – an adaptation. Film versions of books, novelizations of movies, and sound recordings of a song are familiar examples of derivative works. The fact that a work is "inspired" by the old work is not enough to make it a derivative work; to be considered derivative under the law, it must incorporate some of the copyrightable elements of the original work. There's some overlap between the exclusive right to make copies and the right to make derivative works. For example, if a derivative work does not involve some element of original authorship, then it is a copy and infringes the exclusive right of the copyright owner to make copies.

The copyright law gives the copyright owner the exclusive right to "prepare" derivative works. It can be an infringement of copyright to create a derivative work without permission, even if the work is not sold or made public. A work can infringe both the reproduction right and the adaptation right.

● ● ● **Scenario:**

If Leonard buys Karen's book of photographs and then affixes her photographs to dinner plates that he sells, he has created an infringing derivative work. Likewise, if Leonard creates a sculpture from one of Karen's photos he has infringed on her right to create derivative works.

3. Distribution

The third copyright right is the right to distribute copies of the work to the public. The copyright law gives the copyright owner the exclusive right *"...to distribute copies or phonorecords of the copyrighted work to the public by sale or other transfer of ownership, or by rental, lease or lending..."* However, the exclusive right to distribute is limited by the *first sale doctrine*, which is a longstanding rule that permits the owner of any copy of a work to resell, rent, loan, or give that copy away. Under the first sale doctrine, even though the copyright owner has the exclusive right to distribute copies of the work to the public, you can redistribute a copy that you own by selling it, renting it, or giving it away. The first sale doctrine is one of the most basic user rights or privileges in copyright law. It makes it possible to have used bookstores, lending libraries, video rental stores, and art galleries.

Because ownership of a copy doesn't give you ownership of the copyright, you can't rely on the first sale doctrine as an authorization to make a copy of your copy. Nor does it allow you to make a derivative work; to exercise any of the other exclusive copyright rights; or to copy a work that you've rented or borrowed.

⦿⦿⦿ Scenario:

If a bookstore makes photocopies of textbooks available for sale, the textbook publisher's right of distribution is violated. In comparison, selling used textbooks is not infringement because it is an activity protected by the first sale doctrine.

4. Public Performance

The fourth exclusive right is the right to perform the work publicly. The copyright law defines performance broadly to include reciting, rendering, playing, dancing, or acting a work. The law defines "public performance" to include performances at a public place (a concert hall), performances at places where a large number of people are gathered (a hotel ballroom hosting a convention of insurance executives), and performances that are transmitted to members of the public (webcasts, or television, and radio broadcasts). The copyright law contains a large number of exceptions, privileges, and compulsory licenses governing the public performance right, especially as it applies to music.

The exclusive right to perform a work publicly applies to literary, musical, dramatic, and audiovisual works, but not to sound recordings. This means that when your favorite radio station plays a song on the radio, the station needs a license from the composer or the owner of the composer's copyright, but doesn't need a license from the record company or performer who recorded the song. Sound recording copyrights do have a digital performance right, which covers webcasting and other performances of sound recordings over digital networks. So webcasting a musician's song without a license is copyright infringement.

> The exclusive right to perform a work publicly applies to literary, musical, dramatic, and audiovisual works, but not to sound recordings.

●●● **Scenario:**

When you turn on your television to watch a movie being broadcast by your local ABC affiliate, you are "performing" the motion picture on your TV set. Your local ABC station and the ABC network are also performing the movie, as is any cable TV company that is transmitting the broadcast to its cable subscribers. Only public performances are covered by copyright; your "performance" of the movie on your TV set in your living room is a "private" performance and is therefore not something that the copyright owner is entitled to control; the ABC network's performance of that movie, however, is considered "public."

5. Public Display

The fifth exclusive right is the copyright owner's right to display the work publicly. Public display means a display in a public place or a place where the public is, or the transmission of the work to the public. The exclusive right of public display is limited by the first sale doctrine. Thus, the owner of a lawful copy can display it to the public, so long as the copy and the public are within the same room. It's okay to hang it in a museum or show it on TV if the public is in the same room, for example, but you can't broadcast your copy on television or put it on your World Wide Web page. As with other aspects of the first sale doctrine, you have to be the owner, not the borrower or renter of the copy, to be entitled to put it on public display.

● ● ● **Scenario:**

If Karen rents a copyrighted movie for her college film festival project, and she displays stills of the film via the Internet or via her school's cable television network, she has infringed on the right of public display.

Copyright Ownership

There are many different ways to "own" a copyright, but it is very important for artists to understand what kind of ownership they do have, if any. The following sections describe the different types of copyright ownership and the rights and responsibilities that go with them.

Copyright Assignments and Licenses

Once a work is created, the bundle of rights we call copyright begins. These rights belong in the first instance to the creator, although they can be "assigned" - given away or sold - to someone else. The giving away or selling of some of this bundle of rights is often called a "grant." The author of a creative work (or the subsequent owner of its copyright) can make two kinds of grants of copyright rights. The first kind is the **non-exclusive grant of rights** - a license allowing someone else to use the work. This grant may be made orally, in writing, or through an implied-in-fact contract. A non-exclusive grant means pretty much what its name suggests - the grantee can't "exclude" anyone else from using the copyrighted work (including the grantor, who retains most of his or her interest in the work).

●●● **Scenario:**

If Ira writes a letter to the editor of the newspaper or submits an article to a magazine, that's a basis for inferring a non-exclusive license to publish.

The second kind of "grant" is called an **exclusive grant of rights**, and that is an assignment of part of the copyright. This allows owners to make particular uses, while reserving other uses so they can be licensed or assigned to others. Exclusive grants *must be in writing and signed,* just like other transfers of copyright ownership such as mortgages.

●●● **Scenario:**

If James draws a cartoon, he can give the *Village Voice* first publication rights, sell *Funny Times* the U.S. syndication rights, assign *Punch* European syndication rights, give the Acme T-shirt company the exclusive right to make t-shirts, and keep all remaining rights. It is both possible and common to transfer pieces of the copyright. So long as James assigns these exclusive rights in writing, he has assigned those parts of his copyright. If the A-1 T-shirt company should ask him for a license to put the same cartoon on its t-shirt, James won't able to grant that license because he already transferred that portion of his copyright to Acme.

Creative Commons

The Creative Commons (www.creativecommons.org), an organization founded by a number of legal scholars, has developed a series of licenses that allows copyright holders to retain control over their works, but still make them available under terms more favorable than copyright allows. The copyright holder can choose to make the work available under a single license or combination of licenses. For example, a copyright holder can permit use of the work only if it is used for noncommercial purposes and if the work is attributed to him, while retaining the right to make derivative works. Or he could make it available for derivative works, but require that the derivative works be made available under the same terms as the original.

Examples of Creative Commons Licenses

- **Attribution** – Others may copy, distribute, display, and perform your work, and derivative works based on your original, but must give you credit.

- **Noncommercial** – Others may copy, distribute, display, and perform your work, and derivative works of your original, but only for noncommercial purposes.

- **No Derivative Works** – Only exact copies of your work may be made, distributed, displayed, or performed.

- **Share Alike** – Others may distribute derivatives of your work, but only under a license identical to that which governs your work.

- **Public Domain** – The copyright owner dedicates all copyrights to the public domain, for the benefit of the public.

Real World Example: *Special Effects*

In *Effects Associates v. Cohen*,[15] a special effects company sued a producer of low budget horror films for copyright infringement. Cohen had commissioned special effects footage for his movie *The Stuff*, involving aliens from outer space who invaded the earth disguised as frozen yogurt. Cohen was dissatisfied with the footage, but he used it anyway. Because he was unhappy with the quality of some of the special effects, he withheld a chunk of the purchase price. The special effects company sued, claiming that his use of the footage without paying the full price was copyright infringement. Cohen responded that he had commissioned the footage on the understanding that the copyright would belong to him.

The court agreed that Cohen had intended to buy the copyright and Effects Associates had intended to sell it to him. Because they failed to record their intention in a written contract, however, the copyright had not been transferred and remained the property of the special effects company. Nonetheless, the circumstances supported the conclusion that by making the footage and delivering it to Cohen, Effects Associates had granted him a non-exclusive license to use the material in *The Stuff*.

Beneficial Ownership

Anyone who owns one of the exclusive rights that are part of a copyright is legally entitled to sue for invasion of that particular right. The copyright law also grants permits to *beneficial owners* of the copyright, that is, authors who have assigned their copyright in return for a continuing royalty interest. A beneficial owner is someone with a concrete and continuing financial interest in the copyright.

> Beneficial owners of the copyright are authors who have assigned their copyright in return for a continuing royalty interest.

If you sell your copyright for a flat fee, you are not a beneficial owner, even if you haven't been paid yet. Your assignee's obligation to pay you the flat fee is independent of any future exploitation of the copyright. If you are an employee who created works in a "for-hire context," you aren't a beneficial owner either, because your employer's obligation to pay your salary is completely independent of what it does with the copyright.

Beneficial ownership entails only two things: the right to be paid the royalties you contracted to receive and the right to sue third parties for infringement. Beneficial owners have no right to exercise copyright rights, even if they are the original author of the copyrighted work. Their rights resemble those of a landlord; he may lease you an apartment in return for monthly rent, but that does not give him the right to move in with you and your family. It doesn't matter whether your landlord built the apartment herself; she still can't move in with you. Similarly it doesn't matter whether the beneficial owner is actually the author. Once the author transfers the copyright ownership, the purchaser stands in the author's shoes. Thus, the author has no further copyright rights except for the ability to sue for infringement of a copyright now owned by someone else.

Joint Works

If more than one individual created the work, the law will treat them as joint creators. The Copyright Act defines a joint work as one in which the various authors' contributions are created with the intent that they be merged into a single work. Intent is measured from the time of creation and must be mutual.

●●● Scenario:

If Fred writes a symphony and Eleanor thereafter decides to adapt it for a string quartet, that's a derivative work, not a joint work. But the intent need not be manifested in any particular form. It isn't necessary to make a written agreement; courts can infer a joint authorship relationship from the way the two authors behaved when they were creating the work.

If a work is a joint work, then instead of each creator owning a copyright in his or her own contribution, all contributors own a part of the copyright in the entire work. Joint authors are co-owners, and each owns an undivided share of the whole. While each joint author may exploit the work without other joint authors' permission, any profits must be shared with the other joint authors. No single joint creator can give away or sell *exclusive* rights without the other joint authors' participation because the other joint authors are also entitled to license the work.

> Each joint owner can exploit a work without the other joint owner's permission, but any profits must be shared.

●●● Scenario:

If Gertrude writes the lyrics and Harry writes the music to a popular song, both of them own a copyright in the lyrics and music. Harry can give permission for someone to reprint the lyrics even though Gertrude wrote them. Gertrude can give permission for a filmmaker to use only the song's melody as soundtrack music even though Harry wrote the music.

Real World Example: *Disputes Over Rent & Malcolm X*
●●●●●●●●●●●●●●●●●●

Disputes over whether a work is jointly authored frequently arise in collaborative fields such as theater. Courts will find joint authorship where both individuals contributed copyrighted material; where they intended that their contributions be merged into a single, indivisible work; and where they both intended to be coauthors.

Thomson v. Larson, for example, was a lawsuit brought by the musical *Rent's* dramaturge seeking credit as a joint author.[16] Contributing plot elements, characterization, dialogue, and lyrics, Lyn Thomson worked with the playwright and composer Jonathan Larson on the script for *Rent.* Larson died unexpectedly before the play opened, and Thomson continued to revise and rewrite the script. When Larson's heirs refused her request for co-authorship credit and compensation, she filed a lawsuit.

The court concluded that although Thomson had contributed copyrightable material to *Rent,* and both she and Larson intended for her contributions to be merged with his in the script, she was not a joint author of *Rent.* He viewed himself as *Rent's* sole author and viewed Thomson as his assistant. Therefore, the court concluded, Larson and Thomson lacked the intent to be joint authors, and *Rent* was not a joint work.

Similarly, in *Aalmuhammed v. Lee*[17], the court rejected a claim that Jefri Aalmuhammed, who had contributed material to the movie *Malcolm X,* was a joint author of the film. Spike Lee, the director of the film, had followed several of Aalmuhammed's suggestions, but never intended him to be a co-author.

Works Made for Hire

The type of copyright ownership of which artists must be most aware is the so-called "work for hire." Put simply, if you create a work as an employee, that work is considered a "work for hire," and you do not own the copyright. As discussed below, this area of copyright law is complicated and confusing. But for the vast majority of artists, it is perhaps the most important part of copyright law to know.

With "works made for hire" the law considers employers to be the "authors" of employee-created works.

Copyright protection automatically belongs to the "author" of a work as soon as the work is fixed in tangible form. The "author" is not always the person or people who created the work. If the creator of the work is an employee and creating the work is part of her job, then the copyright automatically belongs to her employer. The law considers employers to be the "authors" of employee-created works, which are called "works made for hire."

Sometimes it's difficult to determine whether an individual is an employee for copyright purposes. The courts try to resolve difficult cases by looking at twelve factors:

1. *The skill required to create the work.* In many fields, highly skilled individuals are more likely to work as independent contractors than as employees.

2. *The source of the tools used to make the work.* If the person who claims to be the employer (the "hiring party") provided the tools for creation, that suggests an employment relationship; if the individual used his own tools, that suggests a commissioned, independent-contractor relationship.

3. *The location of the work.* If the work was done on the hiring party's premises, that supports an employment relationship; if the individual did the work on her own premises, that suggests a commissioned relationship.

4. *The duration of the work relationship.* A long-term job is more consistent with employee status; short-term jobs are more consistent with freelance status.

5. *Whether the person who paid for the work had the right to assign other projects to the person who did the work.* In an employment relationship, the employer typically has the right to tell the employee what projects to work on, while an independent contractor is typically engaged only for a specific project.

6. *Whether the person who did the work had discretion over working hours.* That is, if you have to punch a clock, or show up between 9:00 am and 5:00 pm, or otherwise keep regular working hours, then you are more likely to be an employee. If it's okay to work all night and sleep all day, you are more likely to be an independent contractor.

7. *The method of payment.* Employees tend to be paid periodically in salary or wages, while independent contractors tend to be paid in lump sums.

8. *Which party had the authority to hire and pay assistants?* If the person who paid for the work is hiring and paying the assistants, then they are his employees, not yours, and it is likely that you are his employee too. If you hire and pay your own assistants, you are more likely to be an independent contractor.

9. *Is producing this sort of work within the scope of the hiring party's regular business?* If the person who paid for the work is in the business of producing this sort of stuff, then it's more likely that the individuals who actually do the work are employees.

10. *Is the person who paid for the work in business at all?* Those who aren't in business are less likely to be employers than those who are.

11. *Did the person who paid for the work provide employee benefits to the person who did the work?* Both laws and industry practice tend to distinguish between employees and independent contractors with respect to the obligation to provide employee benefits, such as health insurance and worker's compensation.

12. *The tax treatment of the person who did the work.* That is, did the person who paid for the work withhold taxes, contribute to social security, and so forth?

As the courts have struggled with this test, they have tended to give the most emphasis to the last two factors: employee benefits and tax treatment. That makes good policy sense. If a hiring party wants to make sure it owns the copyrights to works that employees create and doesn't want to go to the bother and expense of persuading its employees to execute copyright assignments for everything, the hiring party can treat its employees the way the tax and labor laws dictate. If the employer wants to evade the legal and financial responsibilities that go along with being an employer, it shouldn't expect the copyright law to bend over backwards to give it a break.

If a court determines that the creator of a work is an employee, the employee may still be able to argue that the work performed was not within the scope of her employment – and therefore copyrightable by the employee. Courts will look at whether the project involved work of the sort the employee was hired to do; whether it was created at work or during working hours; and whether at least part of the employee's motivation in creating the work was to serve her employer's purposes.[18]

If the creator of a work is an independent contractor rather than an employee, then she will automatically own the copyright unless she has signed a document that says the work is a "work made for hire," *and* the work fits within one of nine categories:

1. A contribution to a collective work;
2. A part of a motion picture or other audiovisual work;
3. A translation;
4. A supplementary work, such as a forewords, afterwords, pictorial illustration, map, chart, table, musical arrangements, or index;
5. A compilation;
6. An instructional text;
7. A test;
8. Answer material for a test; or
9. An atlas.

The categories are, for the most part, limited to contributions to what would otherwise often be joint or collective works – the sort of works that involve more than one "author." If the creator has signed a "work made for hire" agreement and has created a work within these categories, the work will be a "work made for hire." Thus, the person who commissioned the work will be considered the author.

Calling a work a "work made for hire" has a number of consequences. The employee who actually created the work cannot license the work or sue for copyright infringement. The employer can sue the employee for copyright infringement if the employee later creates a substantially similar work. Although the law gives authors who assigned their copyrights an opportunity to recapture their copyrights eventually, works made for hire are exempt from those provisions.

If a work is not a "work made for hire," the person paying for the work can still demand that the author assign his copyright. In many industries, such assignments are the rule rather than the exception. Copyright assignments must be in writing and must be signed. If you are an artist and want to ensure that your works are not considered "works for hire," the best way to protect yourself is to enter into a contract with your employer (or a person who has commissioned work from you) that allows you to keep some or all of your rights under copyright.

> If you are an artist and want to ensure that your works are not considered "works for hire," the best way to protect yourself is to enter into a contract with your employer that allows you to keep some or all of your rights under copyright.

Real World Example: *Martha Graham*

There are few cases that describe the difficulties of "works made for hire" better than the battle to determine the ownership of Martha Graham's dances. After her death, Ronald Protas, Graham's companion later in life, claimed ownership of the vast majority of her dances, which he then refused to license to the Martha Graham dance studio and school. A federal trial court saw things differently, and found that the majority of Graham's dances were "works made for hire" that she had created as an employee of her pseudonymous studio and school. This decision both elated and upset dancers. They were happy that her dances were free to be performed again, but upset that the copyright to their own dances could be so easily taken away from them. The lesson here for artists whose work is performed as employees: settle copyright ownership issues through contracts prior to creating new works.

Copyright Infringement

Not all uses of protected works require the owner's permission. An unauthorized use of a copyrighted work is legal unless it infringes one of the six legally exclusive rights. Even if it infringes one of the exclusive rights, it may fall within a lawful exception. Copyright owners have, for example, the exclusive right to display their works publicly. The law nonetheless allows anyone who owns a lawful copy of a work to display it publicly to people who are in the same room with the copy. Therefore, owners of paintings can loan the paintings to museums without the permission of the painter and copyright owner. There are many exceptions or defenses to infringement. Fair use is perhaps the best-known defense allowing protected works to be copied without permission.

> Penalties for copyright infringement include monetary damages, injunction or impoundment of infringing items.

Copyright infringement cases involve two different basic fact patterns. In the first fact pattern, it is clear that the defendant has used plaintiff's copyrighted work, but the defendant claims that the copyright law permits the use. This sort of case arises when the defendant claims that her work is a parody of the plaintiff's. In the second fact pattern, the plaintiff claims that defendant copied her work to create an infringing work, and the defendant denies it. In this type of case, courts need to determine whether the defendant's work is an infringing copy.

In deciding whether a particular work infringes the copyright in another work, we have to answer two distinct questions. First, does the circumstantial evidence support a conclusion that the defendant copied from the plaintiff? Second, did the defendant copy the plaintiff's copyrightable expression? Even if we know that the answer to the historical question "Did Marci copy Norman's song?" is *yes,* we need to know whether that copying is infringing. Answering that question requires us to determine if the work that Marci copied can be protected under copyright law. We allow anyone to copy a work's ideas (and its facts, systems, processes, methods of operation, and discoveries). Copying opens you up to a potential lawsuit only if you copy *protected* expression.

●●● **Scenario: Proving Infringement**

To prove that Marci copied Norman's song, Norman will need to show that Marci as defendant *had access* to Norman's song. He will need to show that Marci had *a reasonable opportunity to see or hear* his song. (It isn't necessary to prove that Marci actually did hear or see it.) Then, Norman will also need to show that Marci's song is "*substantially similar*" to his. Something is substantially similar if an ordinary observer would believe the second work was copied from the first. These two facts are sufficient to support an inference of copying.

The burden then shifts to Marci to disprove copying by showing that she created the song independently, or that the similarities between her song and Norman's are not similarities of Norman's copyrighted expression. Marci might show, for example, that the songs sound similar because the same vocalist is singing both. Or, she may show that the songs are similar because they both copy the melody of an older song in the public domain.

Penalties for Copyright Infringement

The copyright owner can recover for actual loss suffered plus the infringer's profits. If the work was registered within three months of publication (for unpublished works, within three months of the infringement), the owner has two choices:

1. Specific monetary damages provided in the copyright law; or
2. Actual monetary damages suffered.

Courts have discretion to award statutory damages of $200 for an innocent infringement up to $150,000 for a willful infringement. Other remedies include injunction or impoundment of infringing items.

Recent Developments in Copyright Law
The Sonny Bono Copyright Term Extension Act of 1998

Seven years after it passed, the Sonny Bono Copyright Term Extension Act (CTEA) is still controversial. The CTEA expanded the length of copyright protection for all works by 20 years. Previous to the extension, the copyright term covered the life of the author plus 50 years. For corporate works and for works created before 1978, the term was 75 years. Its supporters argued that the 20-year extension of copyright was necessary for the United States to keep pace with the many nations, including most of Europe, where terms of life-plus-70 years were the standard. United States intellectual property is our largest export, and our economy could not afford that level of competitive disadvantage, they agreed.

Opponents called the CTEA a dereliction of Congress' constitutional obligation to serve the public interest over the corporate media industries that largely benefited from extension. Detractors pointed to studies showing that up to 98 percent of all copyrights have no financial value to their owners within five years after publication. They also complain that it can be difficult to seek licenses to use copyrighted works because owners often cannot be located.

Some publishers of public domain works, supported by legal scholars, decided to sue to overthrow the CTEA, claiming it violated the spirit and "limited times" requirement of the Constitutional Copyright Clause. They also argued that it violated the First Amendment because it prevented the publishing of works that belong in the public domain.

In January 2003, the Supreme Court upheld the CTEA. The majority said that while the extended term was "perhaps unwise," it was nonetheless temporally "limited" in a literal sense and therefore not unconstitutional. The Court also held that free speech rights were adequately protected through copyright's the "idea/expression dichotomy" (which allows particular expressions to be copyrighted, but not ideas) and fair use. The Court did suggest, however, that it would take a dimmer view of future term extensions.

The extension of copyright terms was ostensibly meant to benefit the heirs of artists, and not individual copyright owners. But the most direct beneficiaries were corporate copyright owners. The public and creators have been the real losers. Their freedom to enjoy and use tens of thousands of works from the 1920s and 1930s has been delayed for 20 unnecessary years.

⊛ ⊛ ⊛ Scenario:

If a dramatist wants to write a play based on Dorothy L. Sayers' classic 1923 novel *Whose Body?*, she cannot do it unless the Sayers estate gives her a license. If the estate chooses not to allow the work, or decides it wants to control the content, or demands a prohibitively high license fee, the dramatist cannot write her play until 2018, 95 years after the novel was first published.

Real World Example: *James Joyce*

Recently, James Joyce's estate, relying on Irish law's 1995 extension of copyright to life-plus-70 years, warned the Irish government that it would sue for infringement if there are any public readings from the Joyce's works in celebrations marking the centennial of Bloomsday in June 2004.

Duration of US Copyright Since Passage of the Copyright Term Extension Act of 1998

Date of Copyright	When Renewal Due	Duration of Copyright
Pre-1932	N/A	Copyright has expired.
1923-1963	During 28th year of copyright, otherwise copyright is expired.	95 years from date of copyright, if renewed in 28th year.
1964-1977	Renewal during 28th year of copyright optional; if no renewal filed, automatic renewal.	95 years from date of copyright.
Created before 1978 but not registered or published.	N/A	Author's life + 70 years or December 31, 2002, whichever is longer.
Anonymous, pseudonymous and corporate-owned works created after 1977 or created but not published or registered before 1978.	N/A	95 years from publication or 120 years from creation, whichever is sooner.
1978 onward	N/A	Author's life plus 70 years.

Under the 1909 Act, works published without copyright notice went into the public domain upon publication. Works published without copyright notice between 1978 and March 1, 1989 have copyright only if registration was made within five years.

Digital Millennium Copyright Act

Congress passed the Digitial Millennium Copyright Act (DMCA) in 1998 to try to address the overwhelming legal and policy implications resulting from the rise of digital media and the Internet. Intellectual property owners feared enormous losses from online sharing and copying. Internet service providers (ISPs) feared crippling contributory and vicarious infringement liability for their customers' actions. Advocates for users warned against stifling the communications revolution with overly protective restrictions on access to and use of information.

The DMCA includes two provisions that are especially important to artists and authors:

- ***Prohibition Against Breaking and Trafficking in Technological Protection Measures ("Anti-circumvention" provisions).*** Perhaps the most controversial part of the DMCA is its prohibition against trafficking and use of encryption-breaking technologies (including software), as well as the publication of descriptions of how to use such technologies. The penalties for doing so mirror those for copyright infringement, but they apply even if no infringement takes place. Thus, for example, anyone who breaks an encryption code that prevents access to public domain works is considered just as liable as an out-and-out infringer. It is also illegal to break the code to play digital media on a platform for which it was not intended (for example, playing a DVD intended for Windows-operated computers on a Linux-operated computer). Nonprofit libraries, educational institutions, and public broadcasters are not subject to the criminal penalties but can only avoid monetary liability if they prove they were unaware that their actions violated the law.

- ***Liability "Safe Harbor" for Internet Service Providers (ISPs).*** The DMCA eliminates ISPs' liability for infringement by their customers if the ISPs remove allegedly infringing works. They must also provide parties claiming copyright with contact information about the alleged infringers. The Act sets forth a relatively simple way for copyright owners to notify the ISP that it is hosting a site containing infringing content. The ISP has five days to remove the infringed material and may only replace it if the accused infringer claims it does not infringe and provides its address and other information, so the accuser can deal directly with the accused.

Copyright owners have little chance to succeed in suing the ISP, as the popular science fiction writer Harlan Ellison found when he sued AOL over its subscribers' postings of several of his short stories. He alleged that AOL failed to remove his works for weeks after he sent notice of the infringements. After years of litigation, much of Ellison's complaint was dismissed, and his only hope of recovery lies in proving AOL was negligent in failing to remove the works promptly.

Congress spent years studying the potential impact of new technologies on copyrighted works and drafting the DMCA. During that time the Internet and its associated technologies continued to evolve and mature, resulting in a bill that is currently archaic and out of date. Most importantly, Congress did not recognize the possibility of peer-to-peer file sharing by individuals. Librarians and other advocacy groups complain that the DMCA doesn't adequately protect legitimate access and uses of works online. On the other hand, corporate copyright holders complain that the law does not give them the tools necessary to aggressively pursue digital file sharers. Several courts recently ruled against the Recording Industry Association of America (RIAA), which argued that the DMCA required Internet Service Providers (ISPs) to give the RIAA the identities of individuals it had accused of uploading copyrighted recordings for peer-to-peer file-sharing.

TRADEMARKS

A *trademark* is a word, name, or symbol used in connection with the sale of goods or services. It is a symbol used to identify products and distinguish them from products made or sold by others. A trademark can be a word ("COCA COLA"), a logo

A trademark is a word, name, or symbol used in connection with the sale of goods or services.

(BUDWEISER beer logo), a picture (the NBC peacock), a slogan (General Motors' "*We are professional grade*"), a package design (the yellow and green design of a box of Crayola crayons), or a freestanding symbol (McDonald's golden arches).

Artists and scholars who seek to comment upon or criticize large corporations or consumer products often face allegations that they have violated a company's trademarks, which are protected under a different body of law than copyright. Thus, it is important to recognize the difference between copyright and trademark.

Trademark Highlights

- Trademarks arise from commercial use.
- A trademark or service mark is owned by the person or business using that trademark on goods or services.
- Trademark law also has a fair use defense, but it is much narrower than fair use in the copyright context.

To own a trademark, you need to use it in connection with the sale or advertisement of goods or services. It doesn't matter in trademark law who originated the idea of the trademark; the trademark is owned by the person or company who makes commercial use of it. Your trademark rights can in theory last as long as you continue to use the trademark in connection with the sale of the product. The rights a trademark gives you, however, are limited. First of all, even if you own a trademark in a particular word, you don't own the word.

●●● Scenario:

Proctor & Gamble's trademark in the word TIDE for detergents does not give it any basis for complaining when people use the word "tide" to refer to oceans. Nor can Proctor & Gamble object when a newspaper reports that people use its product to wash their dirty laundry, a film shows an actor putting a box of TIDE detergent into a shopping cart, or *Consumer Reports* rates TIDE and other detergents for their cleaning power. Trademarks may be licensed for use on other products and may be sold.

Our economy is structured around the concept that market competition in goods and services is the best way to get goods and services people to the people who want them. To promote competition, consumers of goods and services must be able to distinguish between goods and services produced or sold by different entities.

For the producers of goods and services to compete with each other, the public needs to be able to tell them apart. We could accomplish that by establishing an agency to regulate marketing and advertising, but that would be very expensive. We could instead let any consumer who claimed to be deceived or confused about the producer of a product to bring an action, but that would clog up the courts. Instead, trademark law gives manufacturers and retailers a limited property right in their goodwill and reputation and enables them to bring suit on behalf of consumers to stop advertising or marketing practices that consumers are likely to find confusing.

History of Trademark Law

Trademarks initially arose as marks used by craft guilds and their members and developed into marks used to identify the source of goods in the marketplace. Until the mid-twentieth century, trademarks were governed by "common" (*i.e.*, judge-made) law. The common law trademark was a creature acquired by use. If Wally sold Wally's brand widgets on Woodward Avenue, he owned the right to use the mark "WALLY'S" in connection with the sale of widgets on Woodward Avenue. If he wanted to own the mark throughout the city of Detroit, he needed to sell his Wally's brand widgets throughout Detroit. Common law gave the owner of a trademark the exclusive right to use that mark on that particular class of goods in any geographical area where he had used the mark exclusively. Using that mark or a similar mark on the same or similar goods was committing trademark infringement.

When commerce was local or regional, the classic common law regime made sense. The idea was that a trademark was a mere symbol of intangible goodwill that flowed from the public's ability to identify Wally as the source of a particular brand of widgets (even if it didn't know who he was personally). That goodwill only existed in places in which the public had been exposed to Wally's mark in connection with the widgets that he sold. Wally only "owned" rights in his mark in the places he had actually used it. As businesses expanded across state lines, however, Acme cheese from New York ran into Acme cheese from Ohio, so both companies had to adopt different marks to sell in each other's territory.

In 1946 Congress passed the Lanham Trademark Protection Act.[19] The law was intended to establish a uniform set of rules that protected businesses' goodwill in their trademarks and protected the public from deception. The law's substantive provisions were largely a codification of common law principles, but Congress added provisions for a national trademark register that would allow merchants to establish nationwide rights in trademarks without having to sell products in every city and state in the United States.

Basics of Trademark Law

A trademark is any symbol that is used to distinguish the goods of one seller of goods from other seller's goods. You come to own a trademark by using it in connection with the sale of a product. There's also something called a "service mark," which is a trademark for services, rather than goods. Almost anything can function as a trademark in the marketplace, signifying to consumers that a particular product is produced or sold by the owner of the mark.

If it functions as a trademark in the marketplace, it will receive legal protection against uses that are likely to confuse consumers about the source of competing products, whether or not the mark is registered. Registering a mark with the Patent and Trademark Office in Washington, however, allows you to claim it nationwide in any place in the United States where some other person hasn't used it before you registered it.

Trademark Ownership

A trademark or service mark is owned by the person or business using that trademark on goods or services. Imagine that Vic tells Wally that instead of calling his widgets "WALLY'S WIDGETS," he should sell them under the brand name "WIZARDLY WIDGETS." Wally likes the idea and starts selling his widgets under the WIZARDLY mark. Vic then decides he'd like to get into the widgets market and wants to use the WIZARDLY trademark. It seems only fair to Vic that he should own the trademark. After all, he thought of it. Wally, however, is the one who has used the trademark in his sale of widgets, so he's the one who owns the trademark. Disputes over trademark ownership commonly arise when the members of a group that have worked under a particular service mark leave the group.

Real World Example: *The NEW EDITION*

In *Bell v. Streetwise Records,*[20] the five musicians who performed as the "New Edition" claimed that they owned the NEW EDITION mark; their producer and record label claimed that the record label owned the mark and sought to continue to release New Edition recordings performed by a different group of performers. The court concluded that the public understood the mark NEW EDITION to designate the individual performers rather than their record label.

Real World Example: *The Impressions*

In *Cash v. Brooks,*[21] the court resolved a dispute among members and former members of the Impressions, all of whom had been inducted into the Rock and Roll Hall of Fame and Museum. The court held that Fred Cash, who joined the Impressions in 1961 and continued to perform with the group for more than 30 years, owned rights in the IMPRESSIONS name. The court held that Arthur and Richard Brooks, two original members of the group, had abandoned their interest in the name when they quit the group in 1963. Therefore, they infringed Cash's service mark rights by continuing to use the name thereafter.

Personal Names

Personal names may be protected as trademarks if they have "secondary meaning." If consumers have come to understand the name as designating a source of particular goods or services, the name has "secondary meaning" and is functioning as a trademark in the marketplace. There is no absolute legal right to use your own personal name in your business. If using your name on a good or service is likely to deceive consumers about the source of the goods or services you're producing, you may need to change the name of your business to avoid that confusion.

Trademark Infringement and Dilution

Trademark infringement or dilution occurs when someone uses a trademark in connection with the sale or advertising of a product and without the permission of the trademark owner. An unauthorized use of a trademark is trademark infringement only if it causes a *likelihood of confusion* between the registered mark and the allegedly infringing mark. In other words, a trademark owner must be able to show that the infringer's use of a same or similar mark is likely to cause consumers to be confused about the origin or sponsorship of a good or service. In the IMPRESSIONS case, for example, the court held that the use of the name by two unrelated groups of performers would be likely to confuse consumers.

> An unauthorized use of a trademark is trademark infringement only if it causes a likelihood of confusion between the registered mark and the allegedly infringing mark.

Trademark "dilution" is an unauthorized use of a famous trademark that damages the trademark's ability to distinguish the product from other products. Different from trademark infringement, "dilution" does not require proof of a likelihood of confusion, but applies only to marks that are uniquely famous. If someone were to enter the market selling "ZEROX" brand breakfast cereal, consumers would be unlikely to conclude that the cereal was manufactured by the XEROX photocopier company. Because the XEROX trademark is so famous, though, consumers currently recognize the word "XEROX" as having only a single meaning – the company that makes photocopiers and other office machines. The marketing of a ZEROX brand cereal might undermine that distinctiveness and thus "dilute" the XEROX trademark.

Trademark Fair Use

Trademark law also has a fair use defense, but it is much narrower than fair use in the copyright context. Trademark fair use is a non-confusing use of a trademark for the purpose of describing one's own product or the trademark owner's product.

●●● Scenario:

If Nick Kassbaum, who played with the band Steppenwolf in the 1960s, wants to advertise his concerts as by a "former member of Steppenwolf," he may do so even though he doesn't own the STEPPENWOLF service mark.[22]

Truthful comparative advertising is another example of trademark fair use. When Pillsbury airs a commercial claiming that its frozen Toaster Strudel® is more delicious than Kellogg's Pop Tarts®, consumers understand that the two products are unrelated.

Trademark law has no general exception for parodies. Parodies involving trademarks may be open to legal action if they are likely to confuse members of the public.[23] When the parody involves the use of a trademark, the courts will determine whether the use of the mark would confuse the public or dilute the commercial value of the mark.[24] In general, the courts tend to be much less sympathetic to the use of trademarks in parodies that associate trademarks with illegal drugs or pornography.[25]

False Designation of Origin

The trademark law also contains a provision prohibiting "false designation of origin" and "false representations," regardless of whether a trademark is involved. Artists and authors have relied on this provision to challenge failure to credit their contributions.[26] For example, Robert Lamothe and Ronald Jones successfully sued Atlantic Records when it released a recording and licensed sheet music that attributed the music and lyrics of two songs co-written by Lamothe and Jones solely to a different songwriter.[27]

The false designation and false representation provisions have also been used to challenge unwanted credit that might be misleading. Stephen King used the law to prevent New Line Cinema from titling a film based loosely on King's short story *The Lawnmower Man*, "STEPHEN KING'S LAWN-MOWER MAN,"[28] although the court refused to prohibit the studio from claiming that the film was "based upon" Stephen King's short story.

Cybersquatting

In 1999 Congress amended the trademark law to add a specific remedy for trademark owners who discovered that their trademarks had been registered as Internet domain names by "cybersquatters" who intended to take advantage of consumer confusion to attract consumers to their websites. The Anti-Cybersquatting Consumer Protection Act[29] allows trademark owners whose trademarks have been registered in bad faith as Internet domain names to sue for cancellation of the domain name registration. However, they must show that the domain name registrant has no rights or legitimate interest in the domain name. At the same time, Congress added a provision to allow domain name registrants who had been wrongfully deprived of their domain names by the meritless claims of trademark owners to sue in federal court to have their domain name registration restored.

Conclusion

This chapter has sketched the general parameters of copyright and trademark law, especially as they affect artists. The legal provisions affecting creators vary from one creative sector to another, however, and are further complicated by changing technological practices and periodic court rulings. Once a fairly stable body of law, copyright and trademark law are now the object of intense political and legal controversy. New technologies are empowering more ordinary people to become creators; more creators are struggling to find a new balance between their interests as *users* and *owners* of copyrighted works; and new tensions between the public interest and proprietary interests have intensified in recent years.

The most immediate need for working artists is to understand how the law affects them; the following chapters offer a general overview of how copyright and trademark law affect several specific creative fields. But over the long term, the politics of intellectual property law will greatly affect the economics, aesthetics and working practices of most creative sectors. It is therefore important that artists strive to keep up with intellectual property issues and become involved in shaping its future.

●●● ●●●● ●● ●● ●●● ●●● ●●●

Visual Arts and Intellectual Property

VISUAL ARTISTS

Christine Steiner

Introduction

This Chapter contains advice for visual artists in protecting and controlling their work, but also explains why artists must be concerned about protecting and preserving fair use and the public domain. Creativity thrives in a vibrant and massive public domain. It may seem contradictory that the law must protect originality, sanction the reuse of protected works for new creations, and preserve the free use of unprotected materials, yet all are essential for creativity to flourish.

Why are intellectual property issues especially significant for artists today? Artists are both users and creators of works. They use works created by others while at the same time creating original works. Some artists sell products or license images of their works for reproductions. With needs for both access and control, artists may find themselves taking potentially competing positions on issues of free use versus protection.

Visual artists face a special set of challenges as they pursue their work today. One of the most urgent issues is the reproduction and modification of images. While images have been susceptible to alteration or exploitation for some time, new digital technologies and the Internet have made it easy to make and distribute high-quality reproductions of original works. The issues today are therefore different in degree and scope than in the pre-digital era. The unsettled state of the law and artistic practice can be seen in the exponential increase in domestic intellectual property litigation.

Licensing Considerations

A creator who uses the pre-existing copyrighted materials of another has essentially two choices – to use the work without permission and rely on the fair use defense, or to obtain consent from the copyright owner, usually in the form of a license.

Any sale or transfer of a copyright must be in writing.

Licenses are agreements by which the owner of a copyright or trademark lends or gives the right to use the work for a specific purpose. Licenses can be royalty-free or they can be in exchange for a fee – usually a flat fee or a royalty percentage (or some combination of both). Since a license may cover some or all of the rights held by the owner, a licensing agreement should describe the work licensed and identify the specific uses permitted. An oral license to use copyrighted or trademarked material is enforceable,[30] but disputes can best be avoided by committing a licensing agreement to writing. Any sale or transfer of a copyright must be in writing.

Artists will at different times be both licensees and licensors. When creating a new work, artists may wish to obtain a license for the use of a copyrighted work in order to eliminate any uncertainties about whether the particular use is a fair use. At other times, an artist, as the owner of copyrighted or trademarked material, may license works for use by others as a way to earn money and promote her creations.

Artists' Use of Existing Works: Fair Use and the Public Domain

Many visual artists could not function if they did not have ready access to existing works. Two of the most important legal doctrines governing artists' use of prior works are fair use and the public domain. Since the Overview section describes some of the overall principles of these doctrines, this section will explore some of the specific ways that they apply to visual artists.

Many works are in the public domain and are available for use without obtaining permission from the creator. When a work is in the public domain, and freely available for other uses, a reuse of that work will be considered a "derivative work." But to garner copyright in the new creation, there must be sufficient originality in this new work. Changes in the underlying work that courts determine are merely "trivial" or "imperceptible" will not be eligible for copyright. In such cases, the new work will be treated in the same fashion as the preexisting work – as something in the public domain that can freely be used by all. If an artist adds new and original material to the underlying work, the work can be copyrighted – but the protection extends only to the elements the artist has added.

This principle was recently upheld by an influential trial court, which decided that digital images that reproduced two-dimensional works of public domain art were not eligible for copyright protection because the images were not sufficiently original.[31] Although other courts have not ruled on this issue, it may now be settled that mere technical reproduction of two-dimensional works in another medium, without more, will not sufficiently change the character of the new work to make it eligible for copyright protection.

Artists are not just users of the public domain; many actively place their original works into the public domain as a way to encourage its dissemination and re-use. This concept has garnered growing support since the Creative Commons began offering special licenses that allow creators greater flexibility in the use of copyrighted materials.[32]

Besides using works from the public domain or works licensed for limited re-use (through Creative Commons licenses or specific agreements), artists have historically relied upon the fair use doctrine in order to reuse materials that are still under copyright or trademark protection. As described in the Overview, fair use typically entails such uses as criticism, comment, news reporting, teaching, scholarship, and research.

Real World Example: *Fair Use & Food Chain Barbie*

Fair use figured in the court decision on Mattel's 2001 case against photographer Tom Forsythe, who had shot a series of photos of Barbie dolls in a variety of household appliances and food products. By applying the four fair use factors (the purpose and character of the use, the nature of the underlying work, the amount taken, and the potential market effect), the court determined that the *Food Chain Barbie* series parodied the iconic doll and contained legitimate messages about gender roles and consumerism. The court agreed that Forsythe's photos had transformed the meaning and intent of the doll into new and different work. Furthermore, this work did not compete with the original in the marketplace, the court found, because the buying public was unlikely to mistake a naked Barbie in an enchilada with an authorized Mattel product.

> The Internet and digital technologies raise all sorts of unsettling copyright issues.

Relying upon fair use in the visual arts can poses special challenges. Not only must one guess how the fair use test, with all of its nuances and inconsistencies, might apply to a given case, one must do so in the context of rapid technological change and an unsettled body of case law. Digital technologies are affecting the ease and speed of downloading and manipulating images while lowering the transaction costs of distribution. In the meantime, the Internet has made a large mass of restricted and unrestricted images available to anyone. This new environment for visual art means that any web-based materials are subject to unauthorized manipulation, cropping, color changing, and alteration of content. This can make it harder to determine when a digital image differs enough from an original image to be eligible for its own copyright, and whether a digitized reproduction of work in the public domain is eligible for copyright.

The changes in the media environment have raised all sorts of unsettling copyright issues. For example, uploading an image implicates the rights of reproduction and distribution; downloading and printing an image represent two acts of reproduction; and modifying an image potentially violates someone's rights of reproduction, distribution, and adaptation. While copyright law has long made provisions for protecting joint works and compilations, the practicalities of doing so in the digital environment can be complex. In a multimedia project, for example, it can be harder to identify the separate copyright components and more complicated to obtain permissions from multiple artists who have made many separate contributions to the work.

Art-Related Applications of Fair Use
Painting, Sculpture and Other Traditional Art Forms

The first question in assessing whether it is permissible to use another's work in creating a painting, sculpture, or other traditional art form, is determining if the new creation is "substantially similar" to the original. There is no bright line test for determining substantial similarity; many works are not clearly substantially similar or are clearly completely different. Moreover, it is not always clear whether a new work will satisfy the associative standards required to be considered parody of the original.

Real World Example: *Parody & Rogers v. Koons*

One well-known fair use case is *Rogers v. Koons*.[33] Artist Jeff Koons used the photograph, "Puppies," created and marketed by photographer Art Rogers in order to create his sculpture, "String of Puppies."[34] Koons argued that his sculpture was a "parody of society at large."[35] Relying on the standard that the parody must comment on the original work, the court held that while Koons' sculpture may be a "satirical critique of our materialistic society," it was not a parody of Rogers's photograph. Therefore, Koons' use did not qualify as parody and was not fair.[36] The subjective nature of this analysis makes predicting the outcomes of parody cases a difficult proposition. The court found that the sculpture was substantially similar to the original work and therefore constituted an infringement of the photographer's work.[37]

Photographs

Even though photographic images reproduce the factual subject matter they capture, the copyrightability of photographs is a settled matter. Courts have found originality in such creative elements as lighting, placement, shading, balance, and other subjective choices. Generally, the photographer owns the copyright unless the photographs are created as works made for hire or, as discussed above, are not sufficiently original.

> Generally, the photographer owns the copyright unless the photographs are created as works made for hire or are not sufficiently original.

Fair use can be a factor in photographs, as the Paramount Pictures movie poster parodying Annie Liebovitz's photo of a pregnant Demi Moore illustrated (see p. 24). When fair use standards do not apply, stock photography, licensed for a user's specific needs, can avoid legal problems. The stock photographs may be licensed by the owner of the copyrighted work, or by a stock photography company that specializes in licensing photographs for specific uses.

Appropriation Art

Appropriation art, by its very nature, uses the work of another in a different context. The appropriated or borrowed work may be protected by copyright or trademark. The purpose of the use is to alter or comment on the meaning or intention of the original work. It may take the form of reproducing a single image or incorporating many images into a compilation or collage. Appropriation is sometimes controversial because the creator of the original work may not approve of the new work. Andy Warhol was often embroiled in claims by photographers that he had misappropriated their photographic images.[38]

Real World Example: *Barbara Kruger*

Artist Barbara Kruger was sued for her use of a photograph reproduced in the 1960s in a German magazine.[39] Kruger appropriated the photograph, cropped and enlarged it, and transferred the image to silkscreen. She added the words, "It's a small world but not if you have to clean it," in her signature red bold style.[40] The photographer and the subject of the photograph filed suit. The court dismissed the magazine's copyright claim to the photograph because it was in the public domain when used. The court also dismissed the model's right to privacy claim because "Kruger's composite itself is pure First Amendment speech in the form of artistic expression (with sufficient transformative elements . . .) and deserves full protection."[41] Thus, the court protected appropriation as free speech when the new work sufficiently transforms the original.

Appropriation art is an important means of expression for visual artists, one that will certainly continue to generate controversy. The guidelines for free speech, fair use and the first sale doctrine provide some boundaries for the ongoing discussion and resolution of such matters.

Set Design and Background

Art works are often used in film, television, video, and other media. At times a work serves as a central element in the story, and at other times as simple decoration or background. The legality of using a given piece of artwork in set design often hinges on whether the work, as used, is important or trivial. Courts examine whether the use is *de minimus* – meaning that the use is so insignificant that the law should not impose legal consequences or so trivial that it does not result in substantial similarity.[42]

In one case, Warner Brothers was sued for its use of a sculpture and images of the sculptor in the movie, *Devil's Advocate*.[43] Ultimately, this suit was settled by deleting images of the sculptor and sculpture, or by making the images of the sculpture unrecognizable. In contrast, however, another court found no infringement for ten copyrighted photographs that appeared under strobe light during the opening credits of the movie *Seven*.[44] The court found that the use was *de minimus* because the photos were out of focus and not recognizable, even though they were visible for more than 30 seconds.

Real World Example: *Faith Ringgold*

The *Ringgold* case[45] offers an instance where a court found that a work is entitled to protection even if it is used for just a few seconds in the background. Here, visual artist Faith Ringgold's artwork appeared for a total of about 26 seconds as part of the set decoration in a television show. The court found that the use was not transformative because the work was being used in exactly the manner in which it was originally intended – as decoration.[46]

Digital and Multimedia Works

Advances in technology have enabled the inexpensive and easy creation of high-quality electronic copies of visual, textual, and audio work. These copies may be transmitted electronically or posted to an online location. Manipulations may include distorting an existing image by altering the size, color, perspective, or orientation. In order to avoid infringement, the manipulation must result in a new work of sufficient originality to qualify for copyright protection, or it must qualify under fair use.

> When creating a multimedia work, the artist must give careful consideration to whether it will be making fair use of the underlying material

Multimedia works generally involve the compilation of several works into one presentation. This act in itself may qualify as transformative, but the creator of a multimedia work must also be mindful of the layers of protections attached to the various elements used in the multimedia work. For instance, a multimedia creator may need to consider the separate elements of the new work.

Copyright Considerations for Multimedia Work

1. Whether preexisting images are subject to copyright protection, and if so, who owns the rights;
2. If the text is not original, whether it subject to copyright protection, and if so, who owns those rights;

3. For music, both the rights to the specific performance being used as well as the underlying music must be addressed; and

4. Whether any of the words or images are trademarks that may not be used in the context of the multimedia production.

When creating a multimedia work, the artist must give careful consideration to whether it will be making fair use of the underlying material (including whether the new product is sufficiently transformative) or whether the use is likely to be an infringing use.

Websites

The web design industry has exploded in recent years. Software advances have made the cutting and pasting of preexisting materials both simple and efficient, but a creator cannot assume that the content is freely available for use. The issues raised by reuse of that content are the same as are raised in other creative areas if the content of the website is not completely original.

The designer must consider the origin and ownership of the elements that go into the website. Is it owned? Is it new? Is it different? Is it transformed? Each element, including images, text, and sound must be evaluated separately, as noted in the multimedia section above.

Additionally, issues pertaining to linking to other websites must be assessed. Links from one website to another provide an enormous boost to web traffic. By selecting an image or highlighted text, a web user is directed to another page or location. Two main concerns have developed with respect to linking practices: deep linking and framing.

Deep linking is a practice by which a website will include a hyperlink to an internal page of another website.[47] Often this deep linking avoids the other website's introductory pages containing trademarked and other identifying information.

Framing occurs when a link within one website opens into another website, but the content in the second website is displayed within a border or frame from the first website. This practice potentially eliminates the other website's advertising information. It also displays the other website's content in such a way that it may falsely imply a connection between the framing website and the other website.[48]

The courts have generally found that most instances of deep linking, with clear acknowledgment of the source, do not violate copyright law. However, the courts have also made clear that it is important to credit or acknowledge the content or website owner. Deep linking, merely as a link to an inner page of another's website, is unlikely to violate copyright law, but certain uses of linked, copyrighted content (as opposed to providing a mere link) could run afoul of copyright law, trademark law. They might also violate the service agreements that many websites require users to accept.

The legality of framing is less clear. Framing an entire web page is not likely to violate copyright laws because there is no confusion as to the origin and owner of the framed content. Indeed, a court determined that a search engine's framing of thumbnail photos and links to full-size copyrighted photos, with acknowledgment, was a protected fair use. However, framing web page content without acknowledgement, particularly for commercial gain, could lead to copyright liability. For instance, framing a full-page photograph from another website within your website and offering to print that image for sale, would most likely be considered copyright infringement.

Reuse for Purely Commercial Purposes

Although this chapter deals chiefly with using others' works in original artistic creations, it is worth examining the use of another's work in manufacturing products intended purely for resale. In such cases, where there is a clear commercial motive, fair use protections are not as strong. This is *not necessarily* so - courts look at the totality of the matter - but it is important to be cautious where the use is purely commercial.

> The first sale doctrine allows the purchaser of a work to resell, rent, or otherwise dispose of that work.

Reuse for purely commercial purposes raises at least one additional, important consideration: the first sale doctrine. This doctrine (discussed above, on p. 30) allows the purchaser of a work to resell, rent, or otherwise dispose of that work. You can buy a postcard reproduction of a work of art and give it to a friend, but you cannot reproduce multiple copies of the postcard for distribution. In one case, a court found that the first sale doctrine permitted a company to affix notecards of copyrighted drawings onto tiles and sell these decorated ceramic works. In another case, the court held just the opposite.[49]

Given such varying opinions by the courts, it is inherently difficult to assess the legal risks of commercially reusing other people's copyrighted or trademarked work. One may choose to take the risk, after careful assessment, or play it safer by seeking permission through a licensing arrangement.

Real World Example: *Lee v. A.R.T. Co.*

In *Lee,* the court found that the defendant should be allowed to sell tiles to which the plaintiff's artwork had been affixed. The defendant was not making reproductions of the artist's work. Instead, the defendant purchased the artist's work in bulk and then, after mounting the work on tiles, resold the work. The court held that mounting the artist's work onto a tile did not create a derivative work because the defendant did not actually alter the work in any way. Further, the court found that the creation and sale of the tiles was justified under the "first sale doctrine." *Id.* at 581

Visual Artist Rights Act

The Visual Artists Rights Act (VARA)[50] guarantees limited moral rights to the author of a work of visual art.[51] It protects original works, not reproductions, and it provides limited "moral rights" of attribution and integrity. The law provides that authors of a work of visual art have the right to claim authorship of the work; to prevent the use of his or her name as the author of any work that the artist did not create; and to prevent the distortion or mutilation of a work.[52] The rights granted by VARA may not be transferred, but may be waived by contract.[53] Because VARA is concerned with artists' rights as they apply to preservation and authorship of original work only, and in a limited way, this law is not directly germane to the discussion of fair uses of works.

Conclusion

Protecting visual works has become much more complicated and uncertain in the new digital environment. The case law governing fair use and the public domain has always had ambiguities that raised questions about what the law might consider permissible or not. But the law has become especially unsettled in recent years as a result of new artistic practices made possible by digital technologies and the explosion of litigation that is redrawing the legal lines for permissible access and control over works.

PICKING THE LOCK:
Filmmaking in the Digital Age

FILMMAKERS

●●● ●●● ●●● ●●● ●●● ●●●

Vivian Kleiman and Gretchen Stoeltje

Introduction

At the 1992 Sundance Film Festival, Marlon Riggs and Vivian Kleiman premiered *Color Adjustment*, a feature-length documentary film that created a buzz because of its bold reliance on footage acquired without the permission of the copyright owner and without paying a licensing fee. Analyzing how prime-time television portrayed African Americans (from *Amos 'n' Andy* to the *Cosby Show*), the film intercuts excerpts from TV sitcoms with commentary from Hollywood producers and academic scholars. Later that year, the film was selected to launch the new season of *P.O.V.*, public television's showcase for independent film. By the time that *Reader's Guide* announced the program in the weekly schedule, the producers were prepared for the legal threats that ensued.

> Independent filmmakers sit on both sides of the copyright fence – as copyright owners and as members of the public who make use of others' copyrighted works.

Lawyers from CBS and other copyright owners accused the producers of stealing their property. Some demanded a lot of money to license the material. A few threatened to block distribution of the film entirely. In the end, however, no legal challenges were pursued in the courts. *Color Adjustment* went on to garner a George Foster Peabody Award, one of television's highest accolades. The film has been broadcast in several countries, translated into multiple languages, and used to stimulate classroom discussions ranging from media literacy to ethnic studies. Several years after its release, all deferred fees were paid.

This David and Goliath victory was possible thanks to fair use, a section of the copyright law designed to strike a balance between fostering free speech and protecting the interests of copyright owners. Today, that balance is in jeopardy. In response to the birth of digital technology, recent legislation has significantly increased the control of copyright owners by extending the term of a copyright and broadening the scope of activities covered by copyright law.

As independent filmmakers, we often find ourselves sitting on both sides of the copyright fence. We usually own the copyright to our work and therefore should benefit from increases in legal protection. The new laws give us more time to profit from licensing our films to others and offer new legal protections against infringement. For a documentary like *Color Adjustment*, this seems like a good thing. Sitting on the other side of the fence, however, as members of the public who also make use of other creators' copyrighted works, we find our ability to do so curtailed. So although *Color Adjustment* as a finished film may benefit from the new laws, that same film might not be able to get made today without spending considerable time and money on licensing fees and clearance rights.

The digital revolution has radically reshaped the world of media making. But these technological innovations are also changing the rules and practices governing the production and distribution of our work. The goal of this chapter is to familiarize independent filmmakers with critical changes in copyright law and technology that are affecting our work.

Legal Aspects of filmmaking

The art of surviving as an indie filmmaker has always required a certain familiarity with legal issues. From concept to completion, we face the core question of who owns the film: both the film in production and the filmic elements acquired from others that are incorporated into our work. These legal questions are repeatedly subject to scrutiny in our professional publications, most notably the Association for Independent Video & Filmmakers' *The Independent.*

Unlike some other creative arts, filmmaking is frequently a collaborative effort. Before two filmmakers join forces to co-produce a film, they face the task of preparing a partnership agreement that - among other issues - addresses the complicated topic of joint ownership of copyright (discussed briefly on p. 35-36).

To raise production funds, it is common practice to partner with a nonprofit organization that serves as a fiscal agent for the project and enables any donors to the project to take a tax deduction for their contributions. We hire crews to shoot and edit the film, composers to write and record music, and still photographers to document the process. All require either work-for-hire or employee agreements. We prepare exhibition contracts with festivals that have public screenings of the film. And finally, film distributors require contracts that carefully delineate the territory (*e.g.* English-speaking countries only vs. worldwide), the terms (exclusive or non-exclusive), and the duration (*e.g.* three years, five years, or in perpetuity).

Before the film is released, we typically negotiate agreements to license footage and photographs acquired from other copyright holders. Then there's the question of underlying rights and trademarked logos. And if we want to use acquired music, we must request permission from the copyright owners of the composition, the performance, and the recording. This is known as the master use license and the synchronization license.

So the business of indie filmmaking has always been burdened with a nexus of complicated legal concerns. However, filmmakers' increased use of digital technologies and the advent of new laws have raised additional copyright considerations.

Eyes on the Prize:
A Lesson in Licensing Problems for Filmmakers

When filmmakers want to use others' footage or still photos in their films, they have to obtain permission from the copyright owners and usually have to purchase licenses from them. In purchasing these licenses, filmmakers have to decide the extent of the distributions for their films: the longer and more widespread the distribution they desire, the more they will have to pay in licensing fees. Since most documentary filmmakers have limited funding, they often times have to license footage for a limited period of time, a limited distribution area, or for limited (such as educational) uses, instead of purchasing a license that allows for worldwide distribution for an indefinite period of time. Hollywood studios, on the other hand, can afford to "clear all rights for all markets" in their general budget.[54]

The award winning, 14-part series documentary, *Eyes on the Prize,* depicts the struggle by the African Americans for equality during the civil rights movement, is perhaps the most well known example showcasing the possible problems with the current licensing scheme for independent filmmakers. As a result of the high cost of licensing fees, the filmmakers had to determine "what markets to clear their film for…" and the choice is mostly limited by funding.[55] When the filmmakers first cleared the rights for footage used in their documentary, all they were able to afford (and barely) was the minimum five-year license and only for limited distributions. Rights for the documentary began to expire in the mid-1990s, and the renewal process was further complicated by the 1998 death of Henry Hampton, the film's producer. Thus, unless the filmmakers find more funding to renew the licenses (cost estimates are between $250,000-$500,000), *Eyes on the Prize* will be practically extinct: unable to be broadcast or converted to VHS or DVD formats for sale.[56]

Filmmakers' struggles have become worse in the digital age – licensing fees have increased because digital media can better disseminate documentaries to fans, increasing their value.[57] The increase in licensing costs means that the filmmakers of all kinds will have to be extremely careful and creative in their ways to get around licensing restrictions in order to stay within their budget.

Digital Filmmaking And The Digital Millennium Copyright Act (DMCA)

Perhaps the most important of these new laws is the Digital Millennium Copyright Act (DMCA). Like many other artists and copyright owners, filmmakers must contend with the fact that our work, in the form of digital files, is now easier to access, copy, transport, and display than it was in analog form. The DMCA was designed to protect copyright holders against this potential increase in copyright infringement. For an independent filmmaker, however, this law can serve as a double-edged sword.

> The DMCA allows filmmakers to prohibit others from having unauthorized access to their material, but also creates a hurdle that can prevent filmmakers from getting access to others' copyrighted material.

As discussed in detail on p. 46 the DMCA allows us to prohibit someone else from having unauthorized access to our material. But it also creates a hurdle that could prohibit us from getting access to the copyrighted material of others. We often use excerpts from pre-existing copyrighted works in our films and videos. Indeed, it is more often the exception than the rule that films comprise entirely original material. Filmmakers adapt books written by others, use music composed and/or performed by someone else, and edit in footage or photographs shot for another film or for personal use.

Typically, "borrowed" or "sampled" work is legally used in one of three ways:

1.   Licensed from the copyright holder, if the copyright has not expired;

2.   Used without permission if the copyright has expired; and

3.   Protected under fair use, which allows for the unauthorized use of copyrighted material under certain circumstances. However, fair use is limited by the DMCA.

For a filmmaker to make a legal but unauthorized use of copyrighted material, he or she must somehow acquire it. Typically, filmmakers tape programs off television or locate a media junkie with a collection and a willingness to share. A lucky filmmaker may be able to obtain a high-quality copy of the desired program from a studio or network insider who does not mind taking the risk to pass on an illegal dub. Studios, however, are increasingly using copy-protection technology to protect their films from unlicensed copying. The proliferation of digital formats encoded with copy protection means that material will become more difficult to copy and obtain, even if intended for use in a manner that fits squarely within fair use.

The DMCA prohibits the circumvention, or "hacking," of technological protection that prevents unauthorized access to a film or other copyrighted work even if the planned use of the work is lawful.

The DMCA prohibits the circumvention, or "hacking," of technological protection that prevents unauthorized access to a film or other copyrighted work. If a filmmaker chooses to use "encryption," a kind of technological lock that is designed to make unauthorized access and copying impossible, the law prohibits individuals from "picking" that lock. So even a filmmaker planning to stay within the bounds of the law in her unauthorized use of another's footage could still find herself in trouble simply trying to acquire that footage. If the material is in an encrypted, digital format, gaining access to that material in order to copy it (or for any other reason) will break the law.

When the producers of *Color Adjustment*, working seven years before the passage of the DMCA, asked CBS for permission to license *Amos 'n' Andy*, CBS denied their request. Instead of licensing the footage from the copyright owner, the producers acquired episodes of the TV sitcoms in various formats from private collectors of the arcane and home video catalogues, which they transferred to a master in analog format (Betacam, in this case) for editing. Later, when the documentary was broadcast, the project's attorney quickly stopped protests from CBS, explaining how the film's use of the clips came within the privilege of fair use. The CBS attorneys took no further legal action.

Today, however, digital formats prevail, and so does the DMCA. It is most likely that indie producers working today on a film similar to *Color Adjustment* – if they could not afford to pay the licensing fee demanded by the copyright owner or if their request to license the footage was simply denied – would acquire copies of the TV shows in an encrypted, digital format from a local video store. And that would bring the production to a standstill because under the DMCA, the producers could not legally get around the encryption to enable them to copy any part of the footage. While fair use is a defense to copyright infringement, it is not a defense to a suit for circumvention of certain technological protection measures.

Just as the anti-circumvention provisions work to deny filmmakers access to the copyrighted works of others, so should they work to protect the work of that same filmmaker from unauthorized use by others. But the DMCA is really only a useful tool if you can afford to use it. It creates a legal right in support of a technology that alone should provide sufficient protection. But what if it doesn't?

Whether encryption in practice can be an effective deterrent against unauthorized copying is unclear. Many theorize that a technologically savvy person will always be able to invent technology to get around encryption and spread that technology widely to average users. In that case, encryption may not literally protect the work, but only create a new form of liability for those who are able to get around it. This raises a critical question for independent filmmakers: what is the cost of legally stopping someone from using a film? What is at stake in all this, and what would be gained by the effort?

The answer is primarily one of resources and inclination. Assuming that you have the ability to determine that someone is making substantial, unauthorized use of your film, and you have the resources to bring a lawsuit, the anticircumvention provisions of the DMCA give you control that you can exercise. George Lucas, for example, probably has the capacity to investigate allegations of massive copyright infringement, track its effect on one of his markets (all of Asia, for example), and try, through technological or legal mechanisms, to stanch the flow of infringing goods presumably causing him financial harm. For an independent filmmaker struggling to make ends meet, it may not be financially feasible to investigate an act of copyright infringement and bring suit. We may be left, in essence, with a tool we cannot afford to use.

If it turns out that encryption can prevent unauthorized use of one's work, then the filmmaker must ask: is possible protection of my film worth closing off a certain level of access to it? Do I want to protect my work with the same mechanisms that may some day criminalize me when seeking access to the copyrighted work of others?

The Public Domain and The Copyright Term Extension Act

The Copyright Term Extension Act of 1998 extended the term of copyright another 20 years, for a total of the creator's lifetime plus 70 years. The upshot is that an independent filmmaker hoping to use someone else's footage, photograph, or music for free and without permission because its copyright has expired, must now wait another twenty years before the work enters the public domain. Only at that point will the work become available to anyone to use free of charge.

Real World Example: *"Happy Birthday"*

Most of us assume that the song *Happy Birthday* is part of our national folklore and is therefore in the public domain. In fact, the song is a copyrighted work whose owner carefully guards the rights to its use. Like most copyright holders in the music industry, the owner of *Happy Birthday* charges a relatively high fee even for non-profit, educational documentary films. Before 1998, the song would have become available for use free of charge in the year 2010. But the Copyright Term Extension Act will keep the use of *Happy Birthday* out of the reach of many filmmakers until the year 2030.

Digital Film, Education and Copyright

One of the most fruitful markets for independent filmmakers is in educational films. Indeed, the digital aspect of educational video and film has become a booming business. Like everyone else, colleges and universities are beginning to switch their film and video libraries over to digital formats. For now, the primary format is the Digital Video Disk (DVD). Because DVD offers higher quality, extra features, and reduced shelf space, the message from the educational market is that schools want digital copies of the films they buy or have already bought.

The TEACH Act allows schools to use and copy limited portions of some, but not all, films for purposes of distance education only, without first obtaining the permission of the copyright owner and without paying royalties to the copyright owner.

Another reason they are requesting digital formats is for use in distance learning programs. Distance learning is a way of teaching that enables students in different cities, states, or even countries to take classes via computer. Broadly speaking, an instructor can teach the class online both through real-time "discussions" in which the students participate live and by posting class materials on the class site for students to access.

When a teacher wants to use copyrighted material such as a film, she must have permission to do so, just as she would for teaching in a regular classroom. But most filmmakers who sold their films to schools in an analog format did not sell those films for anything but classroom use. The sales of most films predate digital distribution options, so neither film producers nor educational film purchasers thought about the legalities of making films available to students via their computers. Because this is a substantially different way of showing the film to students than the traditional classroom use for which the film was licensed, typically the school must purchase a new license.

In the last few years, schools have begun to establish distance-learning programs and need material for those classes. When that material (a film, for example) was available for purchase in a digital form, such as DVD, the school could simply buy it. Typically, the license that came with that film reflected its release on DVD and the terms set accordingly. But many films were not, and still are not, available in digital formats. Schools then had to make the choice either to eliminate the film from the distance learning class that used it or try to get permission to digitize the analog copy they had already purchased. Although the schools frequently chose the latter route, they often encountered resistance from people who were not willing or able to deliver a digital version of the requested work. The result was a growing gap between what teachers wanted to use in their online classes and what was legally available to them.

Congress got to work on this problem and, in November 2002, passed the TEACH Act (The Education and Copyright Harmonization Act). Essentially, the Act allows schools to use and copy limited portions of some, but not all, films for purposes of distance education only, without first obtaining the permission of the copyright owner (usually the filmmaker) and without paying royalties to the copyright owner.

Filmmakers **unaffected by this law** are those whose films are:

1. Produced or marketed primarily to serve the educational market;

2. Distributed in a digital version; and

3. Not technologically protected OR are licensed to institutions who are authorized to legally circumvent the protection.

Filmmakers whose films are distributed in an analog format only, or whose digital version is encrypted, such that a school can't get around the encryption without breaking the law, receive less protection. In this case, the school can digitize a small portion of an analog version of the film for purposes of distance learning without the consent of the filmmaker and without paying any additional fees.

It must be said that the TEACH Act heavily regulates how schools may make digital excerpts. It recognizes the increased risk of infringement that comes with digital technology and allocates responsibility to the schools at many levels to prevent it. Policy makers, educators, and information technology department staff are all charged with specific duties designed to protect copyrighted material.

Digital Rights, Licensing & Distribution

MovieLink aims to grow the home video-on-demand market for Internet movie rentals. A joint venture comprising Hollywood studios MGM, Paramount Pictures, Sony Pictures Entertainment, Universal, and Warner Bros. Studios, MovieLink charges a fee of $2.99 to $4.99 for private individuals to download first-run and classic titles onto a single computer. That movie is allowed to stay on the user's computer for either 30 days or 24 hours from the time the "Play" button is hit, whichever comes first. MovieLink enforces this license through a software program that controls the file (the movie) once it has been downloaded and ensures that it will self-destruct within the allotted time frame. The license also prohibits copying or moving the file from its originally stored location on the same hard drive, as well as any attempt to circumvent any other security-related tools incorporated into the software.

Choices about the types of licensing terms to apply to a film in a digital format can range from very restrictive models to very permissive. To illustrate this point, we will compare MovieLink, a current online movie rental service, with MovieShare, a hypothetical online video service.

Our hypothetical movie service, MovieShare, operates under a different model. On MovieShare, independent filmmakers offer short films or feature films for download via BitTorrent (and other peer-to-peer file-sharing tools). To download a movie from MovieShare, a movie fan agrees that, if he or she likes the movie, he or she will send $5.00 to the moviemakers through PayPal (or else pay directly through a secure credit-card transaction online). In addition, the movie fan must agree to make the movie available to other Internet users for a certain period of time, regardless of whether he or she likes the movie. That way, the moviemakers have the potential to reach still other audience members and potential donors without having to pay for the extra Internet bandwidth necessary to deliver that content to those other viewers.

How might these licenses look for digital films?

There are numerous ways to combine the available license terms; the range of options is as diverse as the needs of the filmmakers who employ them. For some, it will make sense to restrict the license for a limited time period, for performance only, and for a fee, somewhat like Movielink licenses. Others may want to allow for greater flexibility of use, like in the hypothetical MovieShare example.

For example, a license for film delivered digitally could combine restrictive licenses that apply to certain time periods or for certain versions of a product, with more permissive licenses for the same product during different time periods or for different versions of the product. A similar approach could be applied to several works by one filmmaker or distributed by one distributor: shorter, older, or less popular works could be licensed for a reduced rate when coupled with the sale of a newer product at full rate. The possibilities are many, and some of the choices are not new to filmmakers.

What distribution mechanism might a filmmaker chose?

What is specific to digital film distribution is the issue of copyright infringement and how to respond to it. If you do not believe your film is at significant risk of illegal copying, you can probably feel safe distributing it at your full rate with some encryption protection (just to remind people that your work is not in the public domain and that you still control it). If you are concerned that your work may be subject to significant illegal copying, you might want to issue very restrictive licensing terms that you control with technological encryption, assuming it can provide a sufficient deterrent to copying.

If you don't have confidence in encryption to protect your work, or if you think you can dissuade potential infringers from stealing your film, you can also respond by trying to generate good will. Strategies may include:

- Giving away clips of your film so that people might become interested enough in the whole work to buy it.

- Making your film available under a Creative Commons license, which can permit some copying for non-commercial and other purposes (for more on Creative Commons licenses, see p. 33).

- Making older works available at reduced rates in the hopes of making full-priced sales of newer works.

Who you are, what you have, and your feeling about illegal copying will determine how you choose to license your film.

Conclusion

The coming of age of digital media and digital technologies provide great opportunities for filmmakers to make their creations more widely available. At the same time, the hurdles of encryption, digital rights management, and other technological advances, coupled with stricter copyright laws, might prevent filmmakers from having lawful access to the works of others, which in turn would inhibit the production of new creative works. Finding the balance between access and control will be a major challenge for filmmakers in the near future.

Copyright, Contracts, and Publishing Realities for Authors

WRITERS

Kay Murray

Introduction

Good writing requires skill, and all writing is hard work. That may explain the 19th Century literary master Samuel Johnson's famous quip that "no man but a blockhead ever wrote, except for money." Even if you aren't writing to make money, U.S. law has wisely bestowed on all writers a reward for their efforts – copyright. This law is designed to spark creativity by giving authors a property right in their works for a limited time. By anyone's reckoning today, its designers' objective has been spectacularly successful.

The effects of copyright law on writers are two-sided. The law protects your work from everyone else, and it protects everyone else's work from you. Just as you alone have the right to decide how your work is used and on what terms, so does every other copyright owner. This means that if you want to quote from, copy, or adapt someone else's copyrighted work, you usually (with some exceptions) need permission. Otherwise, you are subject to costly penalties, as is anyone who infringes copyright.

The aim of this chapter is to give creative writers a practical understanding of copyright and publishing licenses, so they can protect their interests, respect others' rights, and be aware when the law is not working as the founders intended. The Overview chapter lays out the basics of copyright law applicable to all artistic genres; this chapter discusses copyright law and processes as they affect writers in particular.

Basics Of Copyright For Writers
Copyright Registration

Although legal protection for copyright begins from the moment of creation, there are many good reasons to register your copyrights with the U.S. Copyright Office. Registration costs $30 and is a simple process. Registration is necessary to sue for infringement. It lets others find you or your publisher on the Copyright Office's website to request licenses. You can register a work any time after it is fixed in a tangible medium, but if done within three months of publication, registration entitles you to attorneys' fees and statutory damages if your work is infringed. Finally, your registration certificate gives you evidentiary advantages in infringement cases.

Established publishers typically register the books they publish within three months of publication. If you send a manuscript to strangers to solicit interest, you'll protect yourself fully from infringement by registering it before sending it. The Copyright Office website (http://www.copyright.gov/) contains complete instructions and the necessary forms.

Fair Use and Obtaining Permission to Copy

Judges have reached different conclusions when applying the fair use test. One judge called it "so flexible as virtually to defy definition." For writers, it can be impossible to predict with reasonable certainty whether a particular use is a fair use. Contrary to what you might have heard, there is no hard and fast rule as to the number of words you can copy "fairly." In a famous case, *The Nation's* publication of some 300 words from Gerald Ford's 200,000-word memoir was found not to be a fair use because the copied passage was considered the "heart of the work." Other courts have allowed substantial copying for "transformative" purposes, such as parody. When considering whether to quote from or copy a work without permission, a writer should keep in mind some of the purposes for which fair use is recognized: criticism, commentary, news reporting, teaching, scholarship, and research. But remember that this list is not exhaustive.

> Because the fair use defense is so unpredictable, always consider trying to get permission to copy or otherwise use a work.

Because the fair use defense is so unpredictable, always consider trying to get permission to copy or otherwise use a work (unless, of course, it's in the public domain.) Unfortunately, permissions can be difficult, even impossible to obtain. You can ask your publisher for help, but most contracts make you responsible for getting permissions. Here are some tips to help you:

Finding the Owner. Registration records for works created after 1977 (and registered) are in the Copyright Office's searchable database (www.loc.copyright.gov). Registrations for works created before 1978 are not online, but are complied in the Catalog of Copyright Entries, available at larger reference libraries. For $75 an hour, the Copyright Office will search its records on a work, including, for pre-1963 works, whether the registration was renewed (if it wasn't, the work is in the public domain).

If you know the publisher, start there. The publisher is probably easier to find than the author, has a permissions department, and sometimes has the rights you need. If it doesn't, it might forward your request or help you find the author. You can also search the Copyright Clearance Center (www.copyright.com) database. The CCC can expedite the permission for works in its repertoire.

To find an author, try the Authors Registry (www.authorsregistry.org), a database with contact information for more than 30,000 authors and estates.

To use song lyrics, you need permission from the music publisher that owns the rights. Try the Copyright Office database or visit the Music Publishers Association site (http://www.mpa.org/Welcome.html) to find publishers and directories of their songs.

Secure Permission. Send a letter to the owner describing your project, the material you want to use, and the scope of the rights you need. Ask if there is a fee to use the work and for the appropriate credit line and copyright notice. Include a permission form that the owner can sign and return. (Samples of requests and forms are available at the University of Texas's extremely helpful Copyright Crash Course website at http://www.utsystem.edu/ogc/intellectualproperty/cprtindx.htm.) Be prepared to follow up and remember that permission fees vary and are negotiable.

If you can't get permission, evaluate the risks of using the work, using the fair use guidelines available. If the use is clearly fair, your risk of suit is small. If the author is dead, the heirs can't be found, and the work is out of print, the likelihood of an owner's materializing and suing is also small.

Exploiting Your Copyright: Publishing Contracts.

Your five rights under copyright are divisible, which means that you can license out one or any combination of them, exclusively or nonexclusively. You can further divvy up each right according to geographic territory, length of time, language, and/or specified format.

Fierce competition to get published leads to draconian contracts in which writers tend to sign away too much control over their work for too long and for too little reward.

Your grant of your rights should be conditioned on the licensee's promise to publish or otherwise exploit your work and pay you a share of the profits from exploiting it. In book publishing, your compensation is generally earned as royalties on every copy sold, and, if you allow the publisher to sublicense rights, as a significant share of the fees paid by the sublicensee. Magazines and newspapers usually offer a flat fee for the rights to articles.

Typically, the negotiation involves the publisher asking for more of the author's rights than it needs, and the author resisting this overreaching. Fierce competition to get published shows no signs of abating as mainstream publishers have consolidated. The result is more and more draconian contracts in which writers tend to sign away too much control over their work for too long and for too little reward. Even with your first book contract, you have more negotiating clout than you know. You should use it. Although the publisher is doing you a service by producing and distributing your work, it couldn't exist without its authors, and it thinks it can profit by publishing yours. Typically, once you've licensed your rights, you cannot retrieve them at will. They belong to the publisher until the license ends (or until you exercise your inalienable right to terminate licenses – which comes into play only after 35 years, or after 56 years for pre-1978 works).

The Book Contract. When a publisher offers to publish your book, it will send you a proposed written contract (called "boilerplate") that is typically long and hard to understand. Following is a brief description of the major terms of a typical boilerplate book-publishing contract.

Even if this is your first book, you should not sign the boilerplate without negotiating. If you have a literary agent, he or she will negotiate your contract. You could hire a lawyer to do so, but be sure she has expertise in negotiating publishing contracts. A better and cheaper option is to join the Authors Guild (www.authorsguild.org). It offers a model book contract and guide and a staff of lawyers to review your contract, explain the terms, and advise you during every step of the negotiation. The National Writers Union (www.nwu.org) is another writers' organization that offers its members information on book publishing contracts.

- *Grant of rights.* You'll be asked to grant the publisher the exclusive right to print, publish, and sell the work in book form, and other print-related rights such as abridgment, book club, reprint, and eBook rights.

- *Subsidiary Rights.* You'll be asked for other rights to exploit the work, which the publisher typically sublicenses out and shares the licensing fees with you. These secondary rights, including merchandising, performance, motion picture, and sometimes foreign rights, are called subsidiary rights. If you have an agent, he or she will reserve some subsidiary rights to you.

Traditional Subsidiary Rights License Fee Splits

	Author's Share	Publisher's Share
Dramatic rights (theatre, movie, TV, radio)	85-90%	10-15%
Pre-publication serialization	85-90%	10-15%
Merchandising	85-90%	10-15%
Multi-media	50%-90%	10-50%
Foreign publication	75%	25%
British Commonwealth	85%	15%
Other Licenses	50%	50%

- *Delivery of a Satisfactory Manuscript.* The manuscript must be delivered on time and satisfactory to the publisher. If it is late or unsatisfactory, the publisher can reject it, terminate the contract, and retrieve the advance. Make sure your contract provides that the manuscript must be "acceptable to the publisher *in form and content*" or "satisfactory in the publisher's *editorial* discretion," not "sole discretion." Set a realistic deadline, and if you agree to extend it, get that in writing.

- *Warranties and Indemnities.* You will have to guarantee that you own the copyright in work and that the work does not infringe anyone else's rights or cause harm. If the publisher gets sued because of what you wrote, you will probably have to indemnify - that is, pay - the publisher for any judgments that result and for its attorneys' fees.

- *Publication.* The publisher should agree to publish your work within twelve to eighteen months of accepting the manuscript, up to 24 months for smaller publishers or children's picture books. Most other details of publication are left to the publisher's sole discretion.

- *The Advance.* Most contracts include an advance, a sum paid in install-ments to the author before the book is delivered that is then deducted from the author's earnings on publication. Advances vary in size, but most publishers won't agree to more than projected royalty earnings on first year sales. Negotiate for the largest advance you can get as a hedge against the risk of low royalty earnings, because you don't have to repay unearned advances. Higher advances encourage the publisher to invest in the book's success.

- *Royalties.* The publisher pays the author a percentage of the price of every copy sold, depending on the format of the book. Typical royalty rates are: for hardcover, 10% of the first 5,000 copies sold, 12 - 1/2% on the next 5,000 copies, and 15% on copies sold in excess of 10,000; for "quality" paperbacks, at least 6%, with an escalation to at least 7 1/2% at 10,000 copies sold; and for mass-market paperbacks, 6% to 8% on sales of up to 150,000 copies, and 10% thereafter. Because eBooks are cheap to produce and the sale price is low, many publishers will pay 25% to 50% of their net profits from eBooks sales.

  Unless the book is deeply discounted at the wholesale level, royalty rates are usually based on suggested retail ("list") price of the book. Deep discount royalties are based on the "net" (wholesale) price – usu-ally 40% to 50% lower than list price.

- *Accounting and Statements.* Most publishers send semi-annual statements and payments accounting for your book's sales, royalties, and license fees earned. Make sure your contract gives you the right to audit the records of the book's financial performance.

- *Out of Print Clause.* The out-of-print clause holds that when the work is no longer available for sale through retail channels and the publisher no longer invests in distributing it, the contract terminates, and the rights revert to you.

- *Freelance Contracts.* In June 2001, the U.S. Supreme Court ruled that periodical publishers' licensing of their freelancers' contributions to electronic databases without permission constituted infringement. A class action suit brought on behalf of all affected freelancers has been in active mediation since the decision.

  Most newspaper and magazine publishers now offer freelance contracts asking for all rights to the articles for a flat fee – no royalties or subsidiary use fees. Despite protests from writers groups, relatively few writers have succeeded in eliminating anything but the worst terms. The Authors Guild helps members negotiate freelance contracts, and the American Society of Journalists and Authors' free "Contracts Watch" (www.asja.org) describes its members negotiating experiences with specific publishers.

- *Work for hire contracts.* The actual creator never has the copyright and may never exploit the work. Work for hire applies in two situations: when an employee creates the work as part of the job; and when a specific category of work is specially ordered or commissioned and both parties agree in writing that it is a work for hire. (For more, see the Overview chapter.) A freelance contribution to a periodical can qualify, but it's rarely in the writer's interests to agree.

  > Be wary of "work for hire" contracts. The 1976 Act makes the party for whom a work for hire is prepared the legal "author" of the work.

- *Protecting Ideas.* Because copyright does not protect ideas, authors with a book proposal or screenplay treatment should try to minimize their risk when submitting unsolicited proposals to producers and publishers. Consider sending a simple contract that provides for payment to you if someone uses your idea. Some companies, of course, won't sign. Some might ask you to sign a release before they'll consider your submission. You can also mail your proposal in a sealed envelope enclosed in a larger envelope with a cover letter that says that by opening the smaller envelope, the recipient implicitly agrees to hire and/or pay you if the idea is used.

> If you have a film or television script, synopsis, outline, idea, or treatment, you should register it with the Writers Guild to document completion date and your identity. You need not be a member to do so. Guild rules apply to producers that have collective bargaining agreements with it. Visit www.wgaeast.org for Writers Guild East andwww.wga.org for Writers Guild West.
>
> Without a submission agreement, you might be able to claim misappropriation if your idea is taken without your permission. The recipient's behavior could constitute an implied promise, as might occur when someone invites you to submit an idea or agrees with a verbal request not to use your idea without compensation. If you send an unsolicited idea, you can only prove an implied promise if the particular industry recognizes the practice.

- *Copyright in Characters.* Literary characters, apart from the stories in which they appear, might be copyrighted, depending on how unique and well developed they are. Even if a character is copyrighted, others may use its general characteristics and the ideas that are associated with it, as long as they don't use the particular expression of the creator. A novel about a superhuman crime fighter disguised as an ordinary citizen doesn't necessarily infringe the copyright in Superman.

E-Books and Other Digital Copyright Issues

In recent years, American publishers have been quick to embrace the concept of "e-books" – digital editions of books that can be read on computers, handheld devices, or special e-book readers – but slow to find or exploit a market for the product. Not least of publishers' concerns has been the perceived need for software makers to prevent would-be infringers from making endless and perfect copies of the original.

But while publishers have been hand wringing over the prospect that their e-books will be illegally copied, Internet-based book pirates have sidestepped e-books altogether, choosing instead to scan the text of traditional paper editions and make the results available on the Internet, often through peer-to-peer file-sharing services. In an exhaustive August 2001 survey, Envisional

Ltd. claimed that as many as 7,300 paper editions of popular books have been scanned and made available on the Internet through distributed file-sharing services such as Gnutella. Among the most commonly traded books were titles from bestselling authors such as Stephen King, Tom Clancy, J.K. Rowling, and J.R.R. Tolkien.

Stephen King has experimented to some extent with the e-book format, but in many ways his foray into e-book publishing, a novella called "Riding the Bullet," led to a product that was more difficult to use (and to copy from) than it would have been if it had been published on paper. In general, we expect computers to make information easier to get access to, not harder, so the limitations on "Riding the Bullet" and on many other e-books are frustrating. (One couldn't, for example, cut-and-paste a passage from King's novella into a high-school essay on the subject — the sort of thing a student would love to be able to do with a digital book — nor could one print it out, since that option was disabled.) This is due primarily to the restrictions traditional publishers place on e-book publishers — or, if they are within the same company, on their e-book publishing divisions.

The practical outcome of the restrictions on proprietary e-book formats is that these formats continue to be dead in the marketplace, at least for now. eBooks are unpopular, considered clunky and burdensome, and, at best, an idea whose time has not yet come. Designers of e-book platforms have been cogitating about the "right" combination of content protection and flexibility, but in the meantime the whole concept of e-books has been languishing. In a world with not enough trees in it — a world in which computer displays are now good enough to give us a book's worth of readable text — this is an unacceptable result.

Conclusion

Because writers often build upon the work of other writers, it is critical for you to become familiar with copyright law and the processes both for protecting your work and for seeking permission to use the copyrighted works of others. As digital book publishing and distribution grow, it will also become important for writers to understand how new technologies can increase opportunities for writers to find an audience, remove gatekeepers, and protect their work from widespread infringement.

●◉●●◉◉●◉●◉◉●●◉●

Intellectual Property Law as Cultural Policy

CONCLUSION

Gigi B. Sohn

Conclusion: Intellectual Property Law as Cultural Policy

By now, we hope that this primer has given you a fairly objective introduction to the basics of copyright and trademark law. While it is important for artists and authors to be familiar with their legal rights and responsibilities, it is equally important for artists and authors to understand how, as a matter of *policy,* copyright law and practice affects them and their work. And it is when we talk about the politics of copyright that we become less objective.

> When they gave Congress the power to regulate copyright, the framers of the Constitution intended to strike a balance between the needs of artists and the rights of the public.

Our premise is simple: that with the possible exception of the wealthiest artists, our current copyright regime hurts artists and authors more than it helps them. The framers of the Constitution, when they gave Congress the power to regulate copyright, intended to strike a balance between the needs of artists and the rights of the public. That balance, discussed earlier in this book, provides incentives for artists to create, and at the same time provides the public with rights of access to their creations in order to promote the spread of knowledge. As the digital age has taken hold, particularly over the past decade, a number of new laws, technological and marketplace initiatives have been put in place that favor large corporate copyright holders over both artists and the public.

These initiatives can be grouped into four general categories, but they all have one thing in common: they seek to make access to copyrighted works either impossible or prohibitively expensive. The consequence has been that artists and authors have found it harder and more costly to engage in their craft.

Longer and stronger copyright

Despite the Constitution's direction that copyright protections be "for limited times," copyright terms have been extended eleven times in the past 40 years; copyrights now extend to 70 years beyond the life of an author, or

95 years for corporations. Longer copyright terms shrink the public domain, making it harder for creative artists to borrow or build upon these works without having to pay licensing fees.

The other significant change in copyright law has been the elimination of such "formalities" as the requirement that copyrights be registered and renewed. As a result, it is often extremely difficult, if not impossible, for an artist, scholar or other potential user of a work to know whether that work is still under copyright, or even who owns the copyright. And it is no excuse for a user of a work to say that they tried to find the copyright. Infringement is a "strict liability" violation, and the costs for such a violation can be expensive – up to $150,000 per instance. This has a colossal chilling effect on creative and scholarly activity.

But changes in the law are not the only way that copyrights have become stronger over the past decade. Perhaps the most significant dilution of artists' (and the public's) rights under copyright has been the shrinking scope of fair use. Large copyright holders typically demand advance permission (and usually a large sum of money) for even the most incidental use of a copyrighted work. Even though use of a work might clearly be considered fair use by a judge, many artists feel that they must change their work, rather than risk the threat of a lawsuit or a significant licensing fee. And many corporate copyright holders, fearing criticism, refuse to grant permission to use their work.[58]

Technological locks and laws that enforce them

While the speed, ubiquity and relatively low cost of digital technologies present greater opportunities for artists to make their works available to a wider audience, they also present greater opportunities for the copyright industries to limit access to, and use of, copyrighted works – beyond what the law would allow. For example, copy protection on certain CDs does not permit them to be played on computers. Similarly, some online music and film services limit one's ability to burn files onto

Copyright law does not permit a copyright holder to tell you how many times you can listen to or read content, for what length of time or on what machine. But "techno-locks," or "digital rights management" tools, permit those very limits.

CDs, DVDs, or hard drives, and others simply cause the file to "disappear" after a specified time period. Copyright law does not permit a copyright holder to tell you how many times you can listen to or read content, for what length of time or on what machine. But "techno-locks," also known as "digital rights management" tools or "DRM," permit those very limits.

As if the technological locks themselves were not enough, the Digital Millennium Copyright Act (DMCA), passed in 1998, ensures that these locks are backed with the force of law. Under the DMCA, it is unlawful to break or "circumvent" these locks, even if an individual's reason for doing so is otherwise lawful. Indeed, the first court case involving the DMCA concerned a Norwegian teenager who broke the technological lock on a DVD that he bought for the sole purpose of playing it on his Linux operated computer.

Techno-locks, backed by laws like the DMCA, have grave implications for creative activity. To the extent that artists often need to study certain works over and over again, excerpt, modify, and transform pieces of works, and play them on different devices, these mechanisms make their jobs not only harder, but also in some cases even illegal.

Licenses that seek to replace copyright law with contract law

Another way that large copyright holders seek to protect their works is through the use of so-called "end user license agreements." These are the icons that you click on when trying to access software or other digital content (click-through licenses), or the terms you agree to when breaking the shrink-wrap on your newest piece of software (shrink-wrap licenses). Without any negotiation, you are asked to waive rights reserved to you under the Copyright Act (such as "fair use") and agree to a list of restrictions, some of which can include a limitation on criticizing the work without the licensee's permission.

Many courts have viewed one-sided contracts of this kind with disfavor, calling them "contracts of adhesion." But in the digital era, these licenses are used to extend the rights of copyright holders beyond that which is permitted by law. Like techno-locks, these licenses can and do limit modification, excerpting, portability, and repeated access to content. As such, they can chill creative activity.

Limits on use of new computer technologies

Peer-to-peer (P2P) file sharing software programs allow a group of computer users to share text, audio, and video files stored on each other's computers. What makes P2P unique and powerful is that there is no central repository of information – the software enables a direct connection between individual computers users. While there are many legitimate business, educational and recreational uses for P2P technology (indeed, it is the technology that underlies the entire Internet), it is perhaps best known as a mechanism by which people share copyrighted music and movies without permission from the copyright holder.

Despite the fact that many copyright holders are currently using P2P networks to sell (or in some cases purposefully give away) their works, the response of the corporate copyright holders to P2P has been to try and make these technologies unattractive to use. They have done so through a variety of means, including:

- Lawsuits against P2P file traders;

- Proposed increased penalties for "making available" even one copyrighted work on a computer network;

- Proposed requirements that P2P software companies provide notice that their networks can be used to trade in copyrighted and obscene materials and that require that such software be downloaded only with the specific consent of the downloader; and

- Proposals that would make legal copyright holders' use of "self-help" technologies that would send viruses into hard drives to prevent an individual from making copyrighted files available to others.

- Proposals that would make it easier for copyright owners to hold technology manufacturers and financiers legally responsible for infringement engaged in by others.

While the widespread use of P2P networks for illicit purposes presents challenges for artists, it might make more sense to work towards finding a way to compensate artists rather than working to hobble or destroy the technology (which is extremely difficult, if not impossible to do, in any case). Some academics and activists have proposed a variety of mechanisms for compensating artists for P2P usage.[59]

● ● ●

We hope that we have convinced you that it is not enough just to know the *law* of intellectual property, but also to know the *politics* of intellectual property. If you want to know more about both, and particularly if you want to get involved in shaping the future of intellectual property law and policy, we encourage you to visit Public Knowledge's website (www.publicknowledge. org) and become part of the network of scholars, librarians, technologists, innovators, artists, and others who are working to bring back the historical and constitutional balance to intellectual property law.

Glossary

Bit Torrent: a Peer-to-Peer (see definition below) distribution technology that permits the sharing of very large files, particularly video files. Files are broken into smaller fragments, typically a quarter of a megabyte each. As the fragments get distributed to the peers, they can be reassembled on a requesting machine in a random order. Each peer takes advantage of the best connections to the missing pieces while providing an upload connection to the pieces it already has.

Compilation: a collection or assembly of existing works. Original compilations may be subject to copyright as a whole, separate from the parts it is composed of, regardless of the status of the individual works.

Copy Protection: technology that prevents certain uses of a copyrighted digital work beyond what the copyright owner wishes to permit. For instance, DVDs use copy protection to prevent consumers from copying or excerpting them.

Copyright: a federally granted exclusive bundle of rights in a work (writing, movie, music, painting, etc.) that restricts others from reproducing, performing, distributing, displaying, and preparing new works based upon the protected work. A work automatically obtains a copyright so long as it is "original" and "fixed in any tangible medium of expression."

Creative Commons: a non-profit organization that makes available to artists and authors a series of licenses that allows copyright holders to retain control over their works, but still make them available under terms more favorable than copyright allows.

Cybersquatting: used to describe the purchase or ownership of Internet domain names, often in "bad faith," usually with the sole intent to hold for resale. These acts are unlawful if the web domain shares a name or close connection with an established trademark and there is "bad faith" or no intent to use the domain for a legitimate purpose.

DMCA: Digital Millennium Copyright Act, passed in 1998. This law prohibits the breaking (or "circumvention") of technological measures used to control access to and prevent the copying of copyrighted works (regardless of possible fair uses). The DMCA also ensures that Internet service providers will not be held accountable for the unlawful actions of their customers.

DRM: Digital Rights Management. See Copy Protection, above.

Derivative Work: a work or creation that is derived from, contains part of, or is based upon an earlier work.

Deep Linking: the practice by which one website posts a hyperlink or link which directs a browser to an internal page of an outside website.

Dilution: a type of trademark protection that does not require any showing of consumer confusion. Instead, dilution of a mark can occur when a famous mark's quality is "blurred," weakened, or tarnished. The dilution concept first arose in the states, but was made part of federal law in the Federal Trademark Dilution Act of 1995.

Encryption: the use of a mathematical/computational process to scramble information so that only those who have the right key or keys can obtain access to it.

Fair Use: the lawful use of a copyrighted work that does not require a user to seek permission from the copyright holder. Fair use often encompasses commentary criticism, education, or non-commercial use. The ultimate determination of whether a use qualifies as a fair use is made by a court using four factors set out in section 107 of the Copyright Act.

Framing: when a link, page, or content from another website is displayed within the borders of the original or first website.

Infringement: unauthorized use of protected material in a manner that violates one of the property (copyright or trademark) owner's rights. In copyright this might involve unauthorized reproduction or performance of a copyrighted work. Infringement can lead to both civil and criminal penalties.

Joint Works: a copyrighted work created by two or more creators with the intent that the final work be one inseparable work. This leads to joint ownership with each creator having the exclusive rights granted under copyright (distribution, licensing, etc.).

Trademark: a distinctive name, phrase, symbol, design, picture, or style used by a business to identify itself and its products to consumers. Trademark rights have historically protected owners from confusing or misleading uses of similar marks.

Peer-to-Peer (or "P2P"): software that permit a group of computer users to share text, audio, and video files stored on each other's computers. P2P permits the direct sharing of files – there is no central repository where files are stored.

Public Domain: the body of creative works, inventions, and other knowledge - writing, artwork, music, science, inventions, etc. - in which no person or organization has any proprietary interest (copryight, trademark or patent rights).

VARA: Visual Artists Rights Act. This law grants visual artists rights of attribution and integrity in original works.

Work-for-Hire: copyrighted works owned by the employer rather than the creator. This arises when the work is created by an independent contractor or as part of an employees' work within the scope of her employment.

For More Information

Books & Articles

Artists, Technology and the Ownership of Creative Content--Creative Control in the Digital Age: Scenarios for the Future. USC Annenberg School of Communication, Norman Lear Center, 2003. http://www.learcenter.org/html/home/?hp=1031775354.

Bollier, David. *Brand Name Bullies and Their Quest to Control Culture.* Hoboken, New Jersey: John Wiley & Sons, Inc., 2005.

Bollier, David and Tim Watts. *Saving the Information Commons: A New Public Interest Agenda in Digital Media.* Washington, DC: New American Foundation and Public Knowledge, 2002.
http://www.publicknowledge.org/resources/publications

Bollier, David. *Why the Public Domain Matters: The Endangered Wellspring of Creativity, Commerce, and Democracy.* Washington, DC: New American Foundation and Public Knowledge, 2002.
http://www.publicknowledge.org/resources/publications

Crawford, Tad and Murray, Kay. *The Writer's Legal Guide: An Author's Guild Desk Reference.* New York: Allworth Press, 2002.

Donaldson, Michael C. *Clearance and Copyright: Everything the Independent Filmmaker Needs to Know.* Los Angeles, CA: Silman-James Press, October 2003.

Fishman, Stephen. *The Public Domain: How to Find and Use Copyright-Free Writings, Music, Art & More.* Berkeley, CA: Nolo, 2001.

Godwin, Mike. *What Every Citizen Should Know About DRM, a.k.a. "Digital Rights Management.* Washington, DC: Public Knowledge and New America Foundation, 2004.
http://www.publicknowledge.org/issues/drm/

Hyde, Lewis. *The Gift: Imagination and the Erotic Life of Property.* New York: Random House, 1983.

Lasica, J.D. *Darknet: Hollywood's War Against the Digital Generation.* Hoboken, NJ, John Wiley & Sons, Inc., 2005

Lessig, Lawrence. *Free Culture: How Big Media Uses Technology and the Law to Lock Down Culture and Control Creativity.* New York: Penguin Press, 2004.

Litman, Jessica. *Digital Copyright.* Amherst, NY: Prometheus Press 2001.

Sohn, Gigi B. *Copyright Reform: The Next Battle for the Media Reform Movement.* Washington, DC: Public Knowledge, 2004. http://www.publicknowledge.org/content/overvies/media-reform/view

Sohn, Gigi B., "Fight for Your Right to Public Domain Art," The Independent, January/February 2003.

Vaidhyanathan, Siva. *Copyrights and Copywrongs: The Rise of Intellectual Property and How It Threatens Creativity.* New York: NYU Press, 2001.

Web Sites
American Library Association, Office for Information Technology Policy. Information Commons Online. http://Info-commons.org.

Chilling Effects Clearinghouse. http://www.chillingeffects.org/

Center for Arts and Culture. The Cultural Commons. http://www.cultural-commons.org/index.cfm

Creative Commons. http://www.creativecommons.org/_

Duke University Law School, Center for the Study of the Public Domain, http://www.law.duke.edu/cspd/

Electronic Frontier Foundation. http://www.eff.org

Public Knowledge. http://publicknowledge.org

End Notes

[1] See *Anderson v. Stallone*, 11 U.S.P.Q.2D (BNA) 1161, (C.D. Cal. 1989)

[2] See *Ringgold v. Black Entertainment Television, Inc.,* 126 F.3d 70 (2d Cir. 1997) ("The central purpose of this investigation is to see, in Justice Story's words, whether the new work merely 'supersede[s] the objects' of the original creation, or instead adds something new, with a further purpose or different character, altering the first with new expression, meaning, or message." (citing *Folsom,* 9 F. Cas. 342 (C.C.D. Mass 1841); and *Harper & Row*, 471 U.S. 539 (1985).

[3] See *Campbell v. Acuff-Rose Music, Inc.,* 510 U.S. 569 (1994).

[4] *Suntrust Bank v. Houghton Mifflin Company* 268 F.3d 1257 (11th Cir. 2001).

[5] *Id.* The court found the new work to be one that "is principally and purposefully a critical statement that seeks to rebut and destroy the perspective, judgments, and mythology of [*Gone With the Wind*]."

[6] For instance in *Harper & Row*, the court found that although only 300 words out of more than 200,000 were taken, it happened to be the most important 300 words in the book. The defendant was deemed to have taken the heart and soul of the book. 471 U.S. 539, 569.

[7] See *Amsinck v. Columbia Pictures Industries*, 862 F.Supp. 1044 (S.D.N.Y. 1994) (stating that the single most important factor in the fair use analysis is that of the effect on the potential market).

[8] *Campbell*, 510 U.S. 569 at 580-81 (stating that if "the commentary has no critical bearing on the substance or style of the original composition, which the alleged infringer merely uses to get attention or to avoid the drudgery in working up something fresh, the claim to fairness in borrowing from another's work diminishes accordingly . . .."). *Id.*

[9] *Id.*

[10] 464 U.S. 417 (1984).

[11] See *Sony v. Connectix*, 203 F.3d 596 (9th Cir. 2000); *Sega v. Accolade*, 977 F.2d 1510 (9th Cir. 1992).

[12] The Court considered the following to be evidence of inducement: 1] Grokster's advertising and marketing, which encouraged the users of the unlawful Napster system to use its network instead; 2] the fact that Grokster did not attempt to filter copyrighted files from its network; and, 3] the fact that Grokster is advertiser supported, and that advertisers paid more for a higher volume of file sharing, which was overwhelmingly of unauthorized copyrighted files.

[13] See *Fred Fisher, Inc. v. Dillingham*, 298 F. 145 (S.D.N.Y. 1924)

[14] See *Alexander v. Haley*, 460 F. Supp. 40 (S.D.N.Y. 1978).

[15] 908 F.2d 555 (9th Cir. 1990).

[16] See *Thomson v. Larson*, 147 F.3d 195 (2d Cir. 1998).

[17] 202 F.3d 1227 (9th Cir. 2000)

[18] See *Avtec Systems v. Peiffer*, 21 F.3d 568 (4th Cir. 1994).

[19] Codified at 15 U.S.C. 1051 et. Seq.

[20] 640 F. Supp. 575 (D. Mass. 1986).

[21] 1996 United States LEXIS 17760 (E.D. Tenn. 1996).

[22] See *Kassbaum v. Steppenwolf Productions*, 236 F.3d 487 (9th Cir. 2000).

[23] See *Anheuser-Busch, Inc. v. Balducci Productions*, 28 F.3d 269 (8th Cir. 1994); *Mutual of Omaha Insurance Co. v. Novak*, 836 F.2d 397 (8th Cir. 1987). But see *Cliffs Notes Inc. v. Bantam Doubleday Dell Publishing Group*, 886 F.2d 490 (2d Cir. 1989) (holding that a parody of Cliffs Notes that was prominently labeled "satire" was unlikely to cause confusion); *Yankee Publishing Inc. v. News America Publishing Inc.*, 809 F. Supp. 267 (S.D.N.Y. 1992) (holding that the first amendment protects New York Magazine's use of a cover for its December 1990 issue that parodies the traditional yellow cover of the Farmers Almanac).

[24] See *Wendy's International, Inc. v Big Bite, Inc.,* 576 F. Supp. 816 (S.D. Ohio 1983); *Deere & Co. v. MTD Products, Inc.*, 41 F.3d 39 (2d Cir. 1994) (holding that the use of an altered deer logo by a competitor in the competitor's advertisements constituted dilution).

[25] See *Pillsbury Co. v. Milky Way Prods.*, 215 U.S.P.Q. 124 (N.D. Ga. 1981) (holding that pornographic magazine's use of Pillsbury's trademark constituted dilution); *Dallas Cowboys Cheerleaders, Inc. v. Pussycat Cinema, Ltd.*, 604 F.2d 200 (2d Cir. 1979) (finding the use of the Dallas Cowboy Cheerleader uniform in a pornographic movie infringing); *Coca-Cola Co. v. Gemini Rising, Inc.*, 346 F. Supp 1183 (E.D.N.Y. 1972) (prohibiting the continued use of Coca-Cola's trademark for a poster showing "Enjoy Cocaine" in the same white script as Coca-Cola's logo).

[26] See *Johnson v. Jones*, 149 F.3d 494 (6th Cir. 1998); *LaMothe v. Atlantic Recording Corp*, 847 F.2d 1403 (9th Cir. 1988); *Smith v. Montoro*, 48 F.2d 602 (9th Cir. 1981).

[27] See *LaMothe v. Atlantic Recording Corp*, 847 F.2d 1403 (9th Cir. 1988).

[28] See *King v. Innovation Books*, 976 F.2d 824 (2d Cir. 1992).

[29] Pub. L. 106-113, 113 Stat. 1536, 1501A-545 (Nov. 29, 1999), codified at 15 U.S.C. § 1125 (d).

[30] *See* 17 U.S.C. § 204.

[31] *Bridgeman Art Library, Ltd. n v Corel Corp.*, 25 F. Supp. 2d 421 (S.D.N.Y. 1988), on reconsideration, 39 F. Supp. 2d 191 (S.D.N.Y. 1999).

[32] The website may be found at www.creativecommons.org.

[33] 960 F.2d 301 (1992).

[34] Rogers had taken a picture of his two friends with their eight puppies. Koons subsequently made a sculpture that duplicated the scene, though he had the images carved into wood and painted in various shades of blue. *Id.* at 305.

[35] *Id.* at 309.

[36] *Id.* at 310.

[37] *See Koons* references at notes 41-44 and accompanying text.

[38] One such dispute that arose when Andy Warhol used Henry Dauman's photograph of Jacqueline Kennedy. See a summary of this claim in *Andy Warhol v. Federal*

Insurance, 189 F.3d 208 (1999). Warhol used Dauman's photograph to create a series of silkscreen prints that were also reproduced many times on merchandise. Dauman sued Warhol, but before the court heard the case, it settled.

[39] *Hoepker v. Kruger*, 200 F.Supp 2d 340 (2002).

[40] *Id.* at 342.

[41] *Id* at 349.

[42] *Ringgold v. Black Entertainment Television, Inc.*, 126 F.3d 70, 75 (2d Cir. 1997).

[43] *Fredrick Hart and The Protestant Episcopal Cathedral Foundation of the District of Columbia v. Warner Brothers, Inc. and Time Warner, Inc.*, Civ. No. 97-1956-A (D.C. E.D., Va. 1997).

[44] *Sandoval v. New Line*, 147 F.3d 215 (2nd Cir. 1998).

[45] *Ringgold*, 126 F.3d 70 (2d Cir. 1997).

[46] *Ringold*, 126 F.3d at 73. However, the court clarified that it in no way intended to indicate that art serves solely a decorative function.

[47] This practice was questioned in *Ticketmaster v. Microsoft*, where Microsoft's site ("Seattle Sidewalk") linked directly to a page that allowed a user to purchase tickets for events. This link avoided Ticketmaster's home page and several pages in between. Ticketmaster complained that this diminished the value of its trademarks and advertising efforts. The case eventually settled.

[48] Not many cases dealing with this matter have reached the courts. Generally, parties will reach a settlement before taking litigation to conclusion through the courts. One example of this is *Washington Post Company, et al. v. Total News*, 97 Civ. 1190 (S.D.N.Y. 1997).

[49] *Mirage Editions, Inc. v. Albuquerque A.R.T. Co.*, 856 F.2d 1341 (9th Cir. 1988), cert. denied, 489 U.S. 1018 (1989). In *Mirage*, the court found that affixing artwork to tiles was not an allowable use.

[50] Several states have similar laws that provide protection on a state level, making the issue of "moral rights" different from copyright interests that are only protected by federal law.

[51] 17 U.S.C. § 106A.

[52] *Id.* at (a) (1) - (3).

[53] *Id.* at (e).

[54] DeNeen L. Brown and Hamil R. Harris, *A Struggle for Rights: 'Eyes on the Prize" Mired in Money Battle,* available at <http://www.washingtonpost.com/wp-dyn/articles/A14801-2005Jan16.html> (last visited Jun 13, 2005).

[55] Katie Dean, "Bleary Days for Eyes on the Prize" available at <http://www.wired.com/news/culture/0,1284,66106,00.html>, Dec. 22, 2004 (last visited Jun 13, 2005).

[56] Dixon, Guy, "How Copyright Could Be Killing Culture," *Toronto Globe and Mail*, January 17, 2005 at R1.

[57] *Id.*

[58] Trademark protection has been made stronger by laws that make it illegal to "dilute the value" of a trademark. This standard has been used to deter social commentaries or criticism about a product.

[59] For some examples, see http://www.eff.org/share/collective_lic_wp.php (proposing a voluntary collective licensing system) and http://www.tfisher.org/ (proposing tax revenues to compensate copyright holders).